Checkmark Books™
An imprint of Facts On File, Inc.

ACROSS THE TOP OF THE WORLD

THE QUEST FOR THE NORTHWEST PASSAGE

JAMES P. DELGADO

Across the Top of the World:
The Quest for the Northwest Passage

Copyright © 1999 by James P. Delgado

Checkmark Books
An imprint of Facts On File, Inc.
11 Penn Plaza
New York NY 10001

Library of Congress Cataloging-in-Publication Data
Delgado, James P.
    Across the top of the world : the quest for the Northwest
    Passage / James P. Delgado
        p.   cm.
    Includes bibliographical references (p.   ) and index.
    ISBN 0-8160-4124-5
    1. Northwest Passage—Discovery and exploration. I. Title.
G640.D45 1999   99-33408
910'.916327—dc21

You can find Facts On File on the World Wide Web at
http://www.factsonfile.com

Originated and published in Canada by Douglas & McIntyre Ltd
Editing by Saeko Usukawa
Text and jacket design by George Vaitkunas
Maps by Eric Leinberger

Printed in Canada

10 9 8 7 6 5 4 3 2 1

This book is printed on acid-free paper.

PAGES ii AND iii *HMS Terror in the Ice*, detail, by **William Henry Smyth** (full image on pages 102–3). National Maritime Museum, Greenwich/BHC3655

PAGE vi **Detail from Thomson's New General Atlas, 1816.** Vancouver Maritime Museum

PAGE vii **Nineteenth-century compass.** Vancouver Maritime Museum

To the people of Nunavut, their ancestors and their neighbours. First peoples of the Arctic, they have always demonstrated how to survive in their harsh, beautiful land.

And for the three most important women in my life: Mom, Ann, and Beth

Contents

Preface

ONE OF THE GREATEST STORIES of exploration and discovery is the European quest for a Northwest Passage—an oceanic shortcut from the Atlantic to the Pacific across the top of North America. In the centuries following Columbus's encounter with the Americas, the search for a route through the continent (as opposed to the long, arduous voyage by way of the tip of South America) engaged the attention of Spain, Britain and other European powers. By the nineteenth century, the quest for the Northwest Passage was a major initiative of the British Admiralty, particularly since it appeared that the passage would lie in British-claimed territory across the more northerly part of the continent. The search for the passage, at that time largely a matter of conjecture and legend, its eventual discovery, and the saga of human endeavour in the far north, are formative aspects of the history and culture of what is now Canada.

After the first voyage of Martin Frobisher to the Arctic in 1576, subsequent expeditions probed the region and its shores, charting and mapping the land and interacting with its indigenous peoples. The climax of this great quest was the ill-fated expedition of Sir John Franklin in 1845–48, when every one of the 129-man expedition died. The search for Franklin and for clues to his fate resulted in the charting of the Northwest Passage by 1859, but it was not until the 1903–6 voyage of Roald Amundsen in the sloop *Gjøa* that the passage was conquered by ship. The final acts in the drama of the Northwest Passage were the two voyages of the Royal Canadian Mounted Police schooner *St. Roch*, which in 1940–42 became the second vessel to navigate the passage, this time from west to east, and again in 1944, when *St. Roch* became the first vessel to navigate the more northerly route through Melville Sound and Prince of Wales Strait.

The frozen north, with its long history of exploration and settlement, the rugged conditions in an environment where survival was tenuous, and the occasional loss of ships and lives in its lands and waters, captured the popular imagination and interest. For people of the Victorian era, in particular, the Arctic voyages of the nineteenth century were compelling. The era of Arctic exploration,

Arched iceberg.
From *The Arctic World*

and the sacrifices it required—isolation privation, starvation, even death—coincided with the rise of the Gothic tale. The accounts of the explorers themselves, culminating in the seventeen contemporary narratives of the search for the ill-fated Franklin expedition, fed the public's taste. Indeed, the high drama and tragedy of the Franklin expedition has probably done more to popularize the quest for the Northwest Passage than any other event. Franklin's epitaph, fittingly enough, was penned for his memorial at Westminster Abbey by his nephew, Alfred, Lord Tennyson:

> Not here: the white North has thy bones; and thou,
> Heroic Sailor-Soul,
> Art passing on thine happier voyage now
> Toward no earthly pole.

The Arctic and its grim appeal have served and continue to serve as muse. Mary Shelley, writing in 1818, when Britain resumed its push for the Northwest Passage, had Dr. Frankenstein chase his "modern Prometheus" into Arctic seas, while Gothic novelist Wilkie Collins penned *The Frozen Deep* about a lost Arctic explorer, drawing on the public's interest in the then still unravelling story of the Franklin expedition.

Artists, too, were drawn by the Arctic and the tales it held. Edwin Landseer, in *Man Proposes, God Disposes*, and Frederick Church, in *Iceberg*, both paint broken masts on ice-strewn shores. Caspar David Friedrich's *Die Gescheiterte Hoffnung (The Polar Sea)* captures the seemingly impenetrable mass of broken, upthrust ice that had thwarted, and occasionally trapped, Arctic explorers. In more modern times, Irish-Canadian artist Vincent Sheridan used the stark images of skulls and of the exhumed frozen bodies of some of Franklin's men to create a series of prints, *A Journey With Franklin*. In several of his prints, Sheridan shows, rising out of the skulls, images of ice-bound ships and desperate men, like long-lost memories embedded within the bleached and flaking bone. Canadian artist Ken Kirkby in his gigantic *Isumataq* depicts the Arctic coast on a 46-metre-long, 3-metre-high (152-foot-long, 10-foot-high) canvas. The scale of Kirkby's work captures, unlike many other paintings, the sheer magnitude of the far north.

The powerful imagery of the Arctic has also inspired musicians. The folk song "Lord Franklin" tells that "In Baffin's bay, where the whale fish do blow, the fate of Franklin no man may know," while Canadian songwriter Stan Rogers yearningly sings:

Ah, for just one time
I would take the Northwest Passage,
to find the hand of Franklin reaching for
the Beaufort Sea.
Tracing one warm line
through a land so wide and savage
and make a Northwest Passage to the sea.

In more recent times, songwriter and performer Sting, in his song "Why Should I Cry for You?", evokes the timeless image of sailing under "Arctic fire" over silent seas, hauling on frozen ropes.

So many words, so many images.

My interest, my passion, lies in the marriage of the two. Ever fascinated by the weaving of words as well as by the verbal texture of memory as it is set down in song or on paper, I have pursued the career of a historian. But at the same time, I have been inexorably pulled by images, places and artifacts. Indeed, in also pursuing careers as an archae-

Sextant, eighteenth century. Used by navigators to locate their ships' positions at sea. It was invented in 1757.
Vancouver Maritime Museum

ologist and as a museum director, I have been drawn to the places and the things we make as humans. In seeking the past, I have tried to meld words with artifacts and landscapes to arrive at a more tactile, if not more intimate, understanding. For me, the past lives because I have been fortunate enough to touch it. This has included wading past muddy banks where the still shroud-encased bones of plague victims tumbled free of their graves beside the Thames, walking over the wooden decks of ships buried in landfill during the California gold rush of 1849, and swimming along the sides of the sunken battleship *Arizona* at Pearl Harbor, past silent portholes with air and oil yet trapped behind them. It has meant picking up scattered bones, opening a hatch last closed by a long-dead hand, silently examining broken dishes and scattered silverware on a galley deck from a Sunday breakfast forever interrupted by a fatal attack on the morning of December 7, 1941.

This personal quest also led me north to the Arctic. It came in stages—first from reading the accounts of the great expeditions, then seeing the Arctic relics themselves—the legacy of the quest for the Northwest Passage. When I was a child growing up in the San Francisco Bay area, my parents took me to see the tiny *Gjøa*, the ship in which Roald Amundsen conquered the passage, nestled in its sandy berth at the foot of Golden Gate Park, looking out to sea. Long after *Gjøa* was plucked from the dunes and sent home to her native Norway, I too took passage from San Francisco. Arriving in Canada, I settled in Vancouver, British Columbia. Now, daily, I see the venerable Arctic schooner *St. Roch* in her concrete berth on the shores of English Bay. Second ship to make the Northwest Passage, this dauntless vessel is now my responsibility as the director of the Vancouver Maritime Museum, *St. Roch*'s final home.

Over the past several years, I have been fortunate to again merge words with artifacts and places as I travelled around the world to numerous museums, seeking the scattered relics of the quest for the Northwest Passage. I travelled north as well, to the shores of the Arctic Ocean, where the stories of the quest played out. This book is the result of those travels and research. It is not

intended to be the final word on the quest. There are shelves of books that examine the various voyages, the personalities and the events. This book, rather, is my attempt to assemble the flow of the story, from antiquity until now, and let the words and the images draw the reader with me along those icy shores.

The Arctic holds many tangible reminders, even centuries after the events discussed in the pages of this book. Stan Rogers sings that the explorers came "seeking gold and glory, leaving weathered, broken bones, and a long forgotten, lonely cairn of stones." The numerous expeditions, the caching of supplies, the building of camps and cairns, and the sinking of ships have combined to create a rich archaeological record. Relics of the Franklin expedition, as well as others, have been gathered by searchers and later by souvenir hunters throughout the last decades of the nineteenth century and for much of the twentieth century. Serious scientific work, conducted under the supervision of the Prince of Wales Northern Heritage Centre, in Canada, has resulted in the documentation and stabilization of a number of sites, and careful archaeological excavation of a few. Fragile and yet strangely resilient, these places evoke the past, be they a ring of rocks that once marked a tent, or the intact hulk of *Breadalbane*, crushed and sunk in 1853

while searching for Franklin and now slumbering beneath the ice off Beechey Island.

In writing this book, I have been privileged to have some experiences that made the past come to life. I have stood on grey gravel beaches, with the wind never ceasing, inside one of those tent rings; floated in frigid waters at the submerged bow of the wreck of Amundsen's *Maud*, and sat in the library of the National Maritime Museum in Greenwich, with the last record of the Franklin expedition in my hands. I have mused, alone for an hour, in the small cabin of *Gjøa*. This book, with its marriage of the words, the places and the artifacts, is my attempt to share a physical sense of the centuries-long quest for a Northwest Passage. For I, like Stan Rogers, sought the Northwest Passage, and found there but the way back home again.

James P. Delgado
Vancouver, British Columbia
April 1999

This imagined scene painted by Allen Young shows *Erebus* and *Terror* wintering in the ice. Young was aboard the yacht *Fox*, commanded by Captain Leopold McClintock, searching for clues to Franklin's fate in 1857–59. Vancouver Maritime Museum

Acknowledgements

THE GENESIS OF THIS BOOK was two research grants made to the Vancouver Maritime Museum by the Department of Canadian Heritage, Museums Assistance Program, for a projected travelling exhibition, "The Quest for the Northwest Passage." While financial and logistical constraints indefinitely postponed the exhibition, this book builds on its storyline and research. This book would also not be possible were it not for the support of the Board of Trustees of the Vancouver Maritime Museum, who have actively encouraged my research and writing since I joined the museum in 1991. In particular, the museum's exceptional W. B. and M. H. Chung Library, which holds the unique Arctic library of Henry Larsen, the skipper of Royal Canadian Mounted Police vessel *St. Roch*, the second ship through the passage, was an invaluable resource. Many times, as I read the accounts of Ross, Parry, Back, Amundsen and the others who sought the Northwest Passage, I was suddenly reminded, when I opened the books to the title page and saw the inscription "Henry A. Larsen, St. Roch, Northwest Passage, 1940–1942," that the very volume I held in my hands had made the passage itself, in Larsen's hands, as he sailed in the wake of the early explorers. I am particularly grateful to the Larsen family for their gracious donation of the library to the Vancouver Maritime Museum.

A number of friends and colleagues provided invaluable assistance, advice, books and shared their own research. I am particularly grateful to: Roger Amy, Chuck Arnold, Owen Beattie, Kare Berg, Margaret Bertulli, Jim Cheevers, Angus B. Erskine, Bill Fitzhugh, Diana Fuller, Dan Gallacher, Barry Gough, Rachel Grant, John Harrington, Bob Headland, James C. Hemill, Francis Herbert, Maurice Hodgson, Jonathan King, Roger Knight, Bard Kolltveit, Harold Langley, Gordon Larsen, Gillian Lewis, Stephen Loring, Timothy C. Losey, Leonard McCann, Joe MacInnis, Robert McGhee, Betty Monkman, Phil Nuytten, Caroline Philips, Rina Prentice, Doreen Riedel, John Robinson, James M. Savelle, Peter Schledermann, Mary Shephard, Ann Savours Shirley, Simon Stephens, James Taylor, Barbara Tomlinson, David Topliss and David Woodman.

The following institutions and organizations were consulted and provided assistance: The Arctic Institute of North America, Calgary; the Bodleian Library, Oxford; the British Museum, London; the California Historical Society, San Francisco; the Explorers Club, New York; the Frammuseet, Oslo; the Glenbow Museum, Calgary; the National Museum of American History, Smithsonian Institution, Washington, D.C.; the National Museum of Natural History, Smithsonian Institution, Washington, D.C.; the Museum of Mankind, London; the Museum of Canadian Civilization, Hull; the National Archives of Canada, Ottawa; the National Archives, Washington, D.C.; the National Geographic Society, Washington, D.C.; The National Maritime Museum, Greenwich; The National Maritime Museum, San Francisco; the National Portrait Gallery, London; the Nautilus Memorial and Submarine Force Library and Museum, Groton, Connecticut; the Norsk Sjøfartsmuseum, Oslo; Parks Canada, Ottawa, Churchill and Calgary; the Prince of Wales Northern Heritage Centre, Yellowknife; the Public Records Office, Kew; the Royal Geographic Society, London; the Science Museum, London; the Scott Polar Research Institute, Cambridge; the United States Naval Academy Museum, Annapolis; the United States Naval Historical Center, Washington, D.C.; the Universitets Etnografisk Museet, Oslo; the Universitetsbiblioteket, Oslo; the Vancouver Maritime Museum, Vancouver; and the office of the Curator, the White House, Washington, D.C.

Portions of the manuscript were reviewed and invaluable criticism and advice offered by Ann Goodhart, David Woodman, Sam McKinney, Peter Schledermann, James M. Savelle and Robert McGhee. Production of the manuscript was made possible by Linda Shore.

My wife, Ann Goodhart, like the exceptional, public-minded librarian she is, encouraged this book, arguing that a new, popular overview of the quest for the Northwest Passage was needed. Fortunately, my friend and publisher Scott McIntyre agreed. The book benefited greatly from the editorial hand of Saeko Usukawa, and the impressive design and layout of George Vaitkunas.

Any errors or omissions are my sole responsibility.

ACROSS THE
TOP OF
THE WORLD

An Archipelago of Ice

There are many memories of hunger in our land, memories new and memories of bygone days. Sometimes famine is due to hard winters with unceasing snowstorms, sometimes to mild winters when the ice will not lie so that the men can hunt the seal at the breathing holes.
—SAMIK, A NETSILIK ELDER, TO ANTHROPOLOGIST KNUD RASMUSSEN, 1922

SOME CALL IT the roof of the world. Others called it *terra incognita*, the unknown land, or *ultima Thule*, the remote north. It is now known as the Arctic. The name comes from the Greek *arktos* (bear), for the region lies beneath the constellation of the Great Bear. An imaginary line, drawn by geographers on the globe at 66° 30' north latitude, marks the Arctic Circle; beyond it lies the top of the world. It is also the location of one of the world's longest-sought secrets, the Northwest Passage. Europe's quest for this passage spanned four centuries. Thousands of sailors and more than a hundred ships participated. The ice of the Arctic still holds some of their bones.

The Northwest Passage—or passages, for there are many potential routes—winds through an archipelago of ice, an intricate maze of islands and peninsulas in the oft-frozen Arctic Ocean. Between land and ice, there is little open water, even during the brief summer. Although most of the Arctic is ocean, it is often frozen, and yet always moving. The ice thwarted most would-be conquerors of the passage. Shifting, drifting, it parted to let ships through, then closed like a trap, imprisoning ships and crews, or crushing them. Or the ice simply remained impenetrable, a barrier as solid as rock, denying access across the top of the world.

Because of the experiences of explorers, some of them ill-suited to and ill-prepared for the rigours of the Arctic, it is popularly known as an inhospitable, deadly land.

The Arctic—and the Antarctic—are the coldest places on earth. Temperatures during the short Arctic summer rarely rise above 10°C (50°F). In the long, dark winters, when the sun never rises, temperatures drop to –51°C (–60°F). And then there is the persistent wind, which can bring a deadly chill. Much of the land is permafrost, or soil permanently frozen to a rock-hard consistency. Because of its barren appearance and

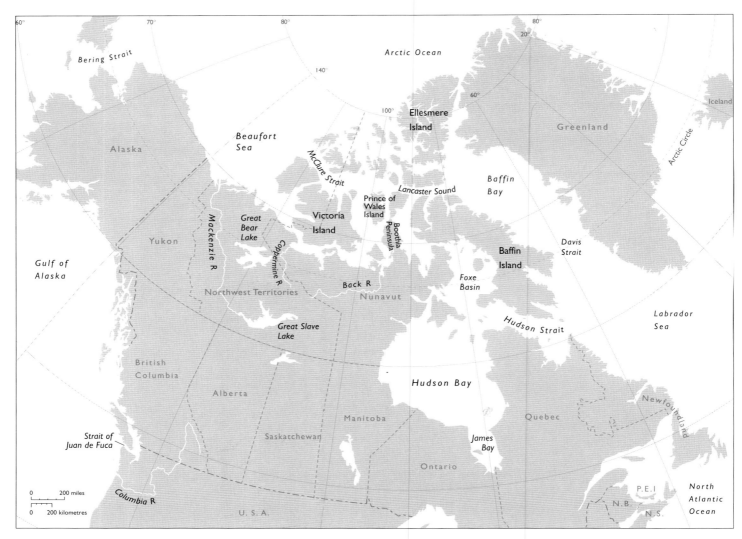

TOP "The top of the world," the Canadian Arctic archipelago and the Northwest Passage.

BOTTOM Sunlight effect in the Arctic regions. From *The Arctic World*

the fact that there is little precipitation, the Arctic is known as a "polar desert."

For a seemingly inhospitable place, the Arctic teems with life. That life is often hidden just beneath the surface, below the ice, or close to the ground, sheltering from the constant winds that whip off the sea and ice to scour the land. The exception comes during the brief summer, when the sun shines for twenty-four hours a day and the land blooms. The melting snow and ice create hundreds of small ponds and lakes; rivers flow, and lichens, mosses, poppies and other plants erupt in bright displays. It is in these small plants that the Arctic demonstrates its complexity. There are more than 2,000 varieties of lichens, 500 types of moss and nearly 1,000 other plant species, each perfectly adapted to this extreme environment.

Compared with other parts of the world, the Arctic's ecosystem is characterized by relatively few species. But within those few species, there may be large populations. Victoria and Banks Islands host over eighty thousand muskoxen. There are millions of seals, and hundreds of thousands of caribou, walruses and whales. The majority of the world's sea birds live at least part of the year in the north polar regions, and the skies are filled with them in summer. There are also insects: spiders, beetles, flies and the ubiquitous mosquitoes that often darken the sky with buzzing clouds.

The animals that inhabit the Arctic divide into two groups; the year-round residents and those that visit during the brief summer season. But all are adapted for the cold. The thick fur coat of the polar bear, for example, is so dense that very little water reaches the skin when it swims in the ocean. The muskox is protected from the cold winds and snow by its long thick blanket of hair and undercoat of dense wool. These year-round residents are joined throughout the long winter by the caribou, the Arctic hare, the Arctic fox and the collared lemming, as well as by the snowy owl and other Arctic birds.

Birds in the Arctic.
From *The Arctic World*

TOP **Caribou migration.** Corel

BOTTOM LEFT **Muskox.** Kitikmeot Economic Development and Tourism, Cambridge Bay

BOTTOM RIGHT **Golden Plover.** Kitikmeot Economic Development and Tourism, Cambridge Bay/R. Wood

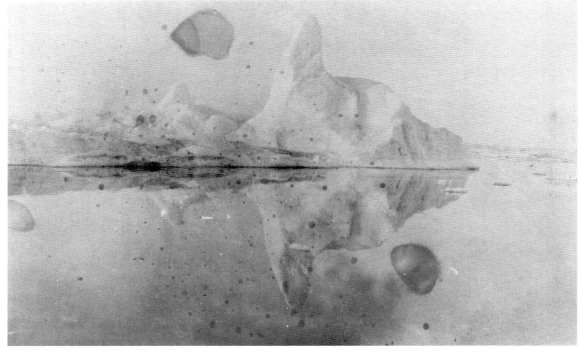

Solid ice, ranging in thickness from 0.6 to 4 metres (2 to 14 feet)—covers about 6,000,000 square kilometres (232,000 square miles) of the Arctic Ocean. Nearly half the surface of the water that does remain open is filled with ice floes. The ice generally drifts southward and eastward, and some of it is carried out of the Arctic and into the Atlantic; this includes icebergs that calve off the west coast of Greenland.

The circular current of the Arctic creates a heavy-pressure ice system in the archipelago and the Northwest Passage, and lighter ice off Siberia. The heaviest concentration of ice, and the gathering place for many ice floes, is the Beaufort Sea, where the greatest average ice thickness is found. Converging ice creates ridges and hummocks in both the Beaufort Sea and in the intricate waterways of the Northwest Passage.

This tortuous, ruptured and riven landscape of ice appears unlikely to be able to support life.

And yet for all its ice, the Arctic Ocean is filled with plankton, which bloom in the brief summer to form an important primary link in the food chain. The fish that feed off the plankton are eaten in turn by ringed seals or walrus.

The Arctic Ocean also supports whales: grays, finbacks, and bowheads, as well as two of the most unusual looking and famous whales, the ghostly white beluga and the long-toothed narwhal. The long, curved tooth of the narwhal grows only on males, gaining length over the years. Early explorers and whalers in the Arctic believed the narwhal was a sea unicorn; early Viking tales of these unique mammals may in fact be the origin of the tale of the unicorn.

The Arctic also supports human life and has for thousands of years. The diverse Native peoples of the Arctic go by different names. In much of Arctic Canada and Greenland, they are Inuit (people); the singular is Inuk (person). In Alaska, they are Inupiat, while in the Mackenzie River delta, they are Inuvialuit. In the past, they were all called Esquimaux or Eskimo, a name given to them by their southern Indian neighbours. They greeted the first European explorers who reached the top of the world.

The Inuit, 1500–1900

By the time Europeans began arriving in the far north, ten major groups of Inuit lived in what is now the Canadian Arctic. Despite their regional differences, the groups spoke a common language, Inuktitut, which allowed for communication throughout the north. The widespread use of Inuktitut greatly benefited explorers who spoke the language, either themselves or with the help of interpreters.

Unfortunately, however, few explorers made use of the ingenious Inuit technology that made survival in the Arctic possible. These included skin clothing, domesticated dogs and sleds, lightweight watercraft and weapons well adapted to

TOP **The frozen Arctic sea.** Vancouver Maritime Museum/St. Roch National Historic Site/HNTN-100-01a

BOTTOM LEFT **Reflection of icebergs.** From *The Arctic World*

hunting not just game but also the sea mammals that were a staple of the diet. Most of their tools and clothing were made from the hides, skins, gut, sinews and bones of the animals they hunted. Wood was scarce; with the average forty-day growing season of an Arctic summer, trees grew less than a centimetre (half an inch) a year in most places.

When Europeans arrived in the Arctic with entire ships made of wood, the display of wealth stunned the Inuit. It was as if, elsewhere in the world, people had arrived in huge ships made entirely of solid gold. The Arvilingmiut, describing their first encounter with British explorers from Sir John Ross's expedition, remarked: "The white men seemed to have such an abundance of wood that they could even live in it—indeed, however incredible it may sound, they lived in a hollowed-out floating island of wood that was full of iron and everything else that was precious in their own country."

Metal, particularly iron, was also scarce. The Copper Inuit of the central Arctic gathered natural copper from the coast near today's settlement of Coppermine and traded it to other groups. But the most valuable metal was iron. The Inuit had small amounts of iron which they obtained from meteors. Also, archaeologists have excavated iron that apparently came from the Viking inhabitants of Greenland; other iron implements were perhaps trade items from whalers who began to probe the edges of the Arctic in the early sixteenth century. Throughout the four-century quest for the Northwest Passage, explorers traded or left iron behind. The Inuit made knives, projectile points and other tools from barrel hoops, files, saws and swords left by the ill-fated Franklin expedition of 1845.

The Inuit demonstrated their adaptability, ingenuity and versatility in many other ways. The key to surviving in the Arctic was proper clothing. Made from the skins of caribou, polar bears, Arctic foxes, dogs, seals and some birds, the elaborate, multilayered clothing of the Inuit

Inuit couple in traditional skin clothing. Vancouver Maritime Museum/St. Roch National Historic Site/HIOS-100-04a

Inukshuit

The Inuit were the first to explore and use the Northwest Passage, but their voyages were to settle and hunt along its shores. As aids to navigation, they erected stone figures, many of them stylized versions of the human form, known individually as *inukshuk* (acting in the capacity of a man) and collectively as *inukshuit*. Their use dates back thousands of years, and inukshuit are still built. They are one of the most recognized symbols of the Arctic.

Inukshuit are also used to mark good places to camp, hunt or gather essential materials, as well as to help hunters drive caribou toward a carefully selected ambush. As the panicked animals run, they mistake the simple geometric forms of the inukshuit for humans or other predators. In this simple fashion, a large herd of animals could be controlled and driven along by a small group of people.

Early explorers often commented on the inukshuit they encountered, recognizing them as signposts. But they were signposts that most explorers could not read, even if they cared to do so. The significance of the inukshuit was learned by the *kablunat* (white men) only after the quest for the Northwest Passage had ended, and settlers, hunters and anthropologists began to ask Inuit informants about the meaning of the "stone men."

Arctic shoreline with inukshuit. Kitikmeot Economic Development and Tourism, Cambridge Bay

conserved body heat, insulated the wearer, controlled humidity, prevented a buildup of internal temperature and was also waterproof.

European explorers were slow at adopting Inuit clothing, often to their peril and occasional doom. The British wore wool uniforms and clothing that made the wearer overheat, and perspiration soaking into the thick wool would freeze, encrusting it with thick ice. Clothing historian Betty Kobayashi Issenman notes: "When their clothing froze and there was no way to dry

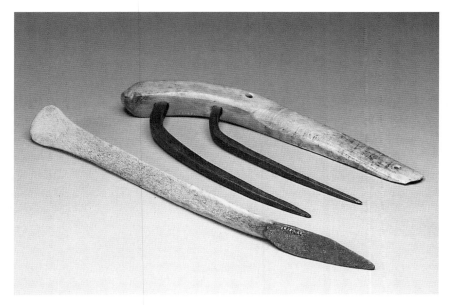

it out, it sometimes became their shroud." Only a handful of early explorers, like Dr. John Rae of the Hudson's Bay Company and Roald Amundsen, the ultimate conqueror of the Northwest Passage, adopted Inuit dress.

Shelter from the weather was provided by skin tents in summer and, for some, in snow-houses known as *igloo* in the winter. Blocks of snow were placed, one atop the other, sloping inward in a spiralling shape to form the dome of the igloo. A ventilation hole was cut near the top

TOP Inuit fish gaff and snow knife. The gaff hooks are made from copper ship's spikes. The knife blade is metal from a salvaged tin can, probably from Franklin's third, ill-fated expedition. Both collected by Henry Larsen aboard RCMP *St. Roch*, **1929–48.** Vancouver Maritime Museum/Michael Paris

BOTTOM Building an igloo. From Parry, *A Second Voyage*

Interior view of an igloo.
From Parry, *A Second Voyage*

and an entrance hole near the ground. Often igloos had long entrance tunnels to help keep the snow and cold air out. As well, groups of igloos were linked by tunnels. Inside the igloo, a multi-generational family would settle in, placing furs over snow platforms that served as a place to sleep, eat and cook. A clear block of ice set into the snow wall of the igloo let in light, which otherwise was provided by a low soapstone lamp that burned blubber and seal oil that soaked into a long wick made of dried moss.

The ability to travel the Arctic's oft-frozen, but also watery vastness was another technological triumph for the Inuit. Using small amounts of wood and skins, they built fragile but eminently useful watercraft. The umiak or large boat was used by some Inuit peoples for whaling and for transporting groups ten to twenty people or possessions across the water.

The more common Inuit watercraft, however, was the single-passenger kayak. A skilled hunter could manoeuvre the light and fast kayak at speeds up to 9.5 kilometres (six miles) an hour.

The Kayak

The kayak dates back to before A.D. 500 and perhaps even as far back as 2000 B.C. Usually built for a single passenger, the kayak was generally used only by men to hunt sea mammals, waterfowl, or moose and caribou swimming in shallows. Long and narrow, sharp ended, low-sided and completely covered with skin except for a small hatch where the hunter sits, the kayak was propelled with a single double-bladed paddle. The frame was of driftwood and bone pegged and lashed together. It took five caribou or nine seal skins to cover the average kayak. The skin was usually replaced every year. Seal oil was used to waterproof the skin.

Because of the light, fragile nature of kayaks, only a few fragments of early ones have survived. To find evidence of ancient kayaks, archaeologists look for sea mammal bones and harpoon parts (both of which indicate hunting on the water), as well as small wood and ivory models of kayaks. These models appear to have been charms to ensure safe use of kayaks, which capsize easily.

Early European explorers in the Arctic frequently commented on the skin boats used by Inuit peoples. The Inuit continued to build and use kayaks until the mid-nineteenth century, when cultural disruption and the availability of commercially made canoes and boats took the place of traditional skin-covered watercraft.

Hunting in kayaks.
From Parry, *A Second Voyage*

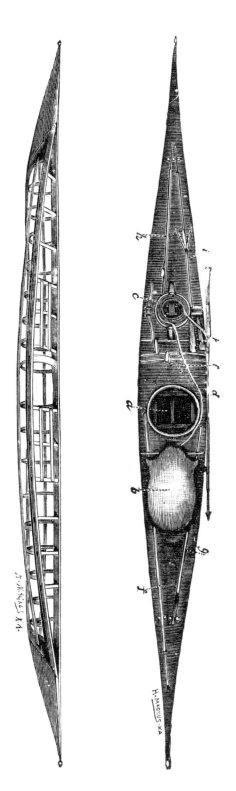

Views of a kayak.
From Nansen, *Eskimo Life*

The dog and the dogsled joined the kayak as indispensable tools. Dogsleds, known as *komatik*, were made of wood, whalebone, baleen, even frozen hides and skins. Long and narrow, they could carry heavy loads and were pulled by a team of six to twelve dogs. Sleds were built to be flexible, to bend and give as they rode over the uneven surface of the snow and ice. The long runners, curved at the front, were coated with mud. When the mud froze, it enabled the runners to glide over the ice with ease. The Inuit taught this trick to explorers; the crew of the RCMP vessel *St. Roch*, in the 1930s, coated their sled runners with frozen oatmeal. When they ran short of food on patrol, they thawed the oatmeal and ate it.

The Inuit and their dogs had a close relationship. Dogs were trained to be good pullers, fighters and hunters. The Inuit would suck the nostrils of a dog from time to time to give it a "good sense of smell and easily get the scent of seal breathing holes," according to anthropologist Knud Rasmussen.

The dog introduced a new story into Inuit mythology. When the Inuit first met *kablunat*

Kayak Hunter's Song

Anthropologist and explorer Knud Rasmussen recorded an elderly Netsilik hunter's song about his kayak and published it in 1930. Rasmussen "expanded" his translation to incorporate some of the composer's explanations of his song:	I call to mind And think of the early coming of spring As I knew it In my younger days. Was I ever such a hunter! Was it myself indeed? For I see And recall in memory a man in a kayak: Slowly he toils along in toward the shores of the lake; With many spear-slain caribou in tow. Happiest am I In my memories of hunting in a kayak. On land, I was never of great renown Among the herds of caribou. And an old man, seeking strength in his youth Loves most to think of the deed Whereby he gained renown.

LEFT Toggled harpoon head.
From Nansen, *Eskimo Life*

BELOW Inuit man named Manuak, wearing snow goggles, 1935–37. Vancouver Maritime Museum/St. Roch National Historic Site/Frank Willan Collection/HIOS-30-10a

(white men), they were at a loss to explain who these different people were and where they came from. Finally, they decided that the kablunat's origins were found in an old tale of an arrogant, disobedient girl who lay with a dog. The kablunat were the offspring of that union.

Inuit weapons for hunting included built-up bows made of pieces of wood, lashed together and reinforced with sinew, and lances, spears and harpoons with detachable toggled heads. A line attached the spear head to the shaft, allowing the hunter to haul in his catch. Harpoons for whaling used the same technology, as did some arrows.

Inuit usually ate their food raw: seal liver, blubber and meat, as well as whale, provided essential nutrients and vitamins to ensure health. Other foods included blood soup and partially digested plants or shrimp from the stomachs of birds and animals killed by hunters. All drinking water came from melting snow or ice.

Snow Goggles

The intense sunlight of springtime, when reflected from the snow-covered ground, causes a temporary condition called snow blindness. To prevent this, the Inuit made snow goggles. These were fashioned to fit the contours of the face snugly to allow light to enter only through narrow slits that restricted the field of vision, reducing the amount of light reaching the optic nerve. The width of the slits governs the width of lateral vision, and the narrower the slit, the more acuity of vision. The area behind each slit is hollowed out to prevent eye contact and blackened to eliminate glare. This pair of snow goggles is made of antler; others were made of wood, bone or ivory.

Snow goggles made of antler, collected by Henry Larsen aboard the Royal Canadian Mounted Police schooner *St. Roch*, 1929–48. Vancouver Maritime Museum/Michael Paris.

Life was difficult and survival was never assured in the Arctic. Netsilik elder Quqortingneq told anthropologist Knud Rasmussen: "Life is so with us that we are never surprised when we hear that someone has starved to death. We are so used to it. It sometimes happens to the best of us."

For the Inuit, the world, including that under the sea, was a mystical place filled with spirits and supernatural beings. Taboo was an important means of protection. To avoid angering spirits, land and sea animals could not be eaten on the same day; weapons used to hunt sea mammals, if they had been used on land, required purification in the smoke of a seaweed fire. Amulets also provided some protection, as did the intervention of shamans and magic words. Some shamans could shift their shape and become bears, seals, or other animals. The intricate system of belief, superstition and ritual helped the Inuit to survive and to explain things they might not otherwise understand, like the coming of the kablunat. Inuit stories stretch far back into the past, and not even they are quite sure when the first *kabluna* (white person) reached the Arctic.

Ultima Thule

Arctic waters may have been reached as early as 330–300 B.C. by Pytheas of Massalia, a Greek geographer, who apparently sailed as far north as Scandinavia or beyond. The account of his voyage has not survived, but later writers, like Pliny and Strabo, drew from it to write about a place six days' sail north of Britain. One day farther north, Pliny writes of a "congealed" or "frozen ocean" where the sun was visible twenty-four hours a day. The name of this place was Thule. No one is certain where Thule was (possibly Iceland or northern Norway) and how much of the accounts are true, but the mention of frozen seas and constant daylight does indicate a northern clime.

Inuit drum dancers.
From Parry, *A Second Voyage*

Irish monks may also have reached the sub-Arctic or Arctic in ancient times; the monk Dicuil noted in A.D. 825 that thirty years hence priests had lived on an island in the north, where during the summer the sun never fully set, and "a day's sail northward from it they found the frozen sea."

The first Europeans known to encounter the Arctic were the Norse, or Vikings, voyaging west and north out of Scandinavia. Reaching Iceland in A.D. 860, they pushed farther west in 982 when Eirik Thorvaldsson Raudi, "Erik the Red," sailed to Greenland's shores. Within a few decades, two Norse colonies with several thousand inhabitants sprang up on the eastern and western shores of Greenland. By 1267, and possibly earlier, Norse navigators were venturing up past the Arctic Circle to the shores of Ellesmere Island at 76° north latitude. They even sailed the 320-kilometre (200-mile) distance across Davis Strait to reach Baffin Island.

The Vikings knew the lands around Disko Bay in Greenland as Nordrsetur, a place where they hunted in summer. The settlers hunted Arctic game, exporting to Europe walrus ivory and hides, live polar bears and narwhal tusks, identified as "unicorn horns." Traces of the Norse have been found even farther north. In 1824, an Inuk named Pelimut discovered three stone cairns on the island of Kingigtorssuaq, at latitude 73°, north of the Arctic Circle. In one cairn was a small stone, carved with Norse runes, that told of three hunters erecting the cairns in late April, sometime in the early fourteenth century.

In 1978–79, archaeologist Peter Schledermann, excavating a thirteenth-century Inuit settlement on Skraeling Island, off Ellesmere Island in northern Baffin Bay, discovered "more than fifty items of Norse origin." They included pieces of woollen cloth, fragments of chain mail, ship rivets, knife and spear blades, a carpenter's plane, pieces of a wooden barrel and a gaming piece. Radiocarbon dating places these artifacts between A.D. 1200 and 1260. Schledermann believes that one or more Norse vessels entered the upper regions of Baffin Bay

On Skraeling Island, off the coast of Ellesmere Island, archaeologist Peter Schledermann found traces of contact between Inuit and the Norse while excavating an abandoned Inuit house site. Peter Schledermann

late in the thirteenth century "on a voyage of exploration," sailing north close to the coast of Ellesmere Island. "Their vessel or vessels may have been crushed in the ice," he writes, with survivors living among the Inuit at the site he excavated. Or they may have stopped for the winter before sailing south to safety.

Other Inuit sites have also yielded Norse artifacts. A piece of a bronze balance was found on the west coast of Ellesmere Island by archaeologist Patricia Sutherland. More tantalizing fragments of metal have been discovered on Hudson Bay, and on Devon and Bathurst Islands. Some of the Norse metal, a valuable commodity, was doubtless acquired in trade between groups of Inuit or even through direct contact. There is evidence that hints of face-to-face contact. An Inuit figure from Baffin Island depicts a Viking, as does another six-hundred-year-old, wooden figure from northern Greenland. Schledermann's team also found a carved piece of driftwood with "the facial features of a distinctly non-Inuit person."

The Norse presence in the Arctic and sub-Arctic diminished with the onset of the last Little Ice Age around 1250. The next few centuries saw temperatures dropping, ice moving farther south and winters becoming harsher. The Inuit were also moving south and by 1200 had reached Disko. Viking and Inuit accounts both speak of clashes and bloodshed. Strife with *skraeling* (the Viking term for the Inuit) and with each other, doomed the western Norse settlements by 1450. Within decades, the last reliable accounts of the Norse in Greenland trickle out into silence. Inuit tales suggest that some Norse, notably women and children, settled with them, fuelling speculation among later explorers and anthropologists over the origins of "fair" Inuit they encountered.

TOP Viking ship rivet excavated from an Inuit site on Skraeling Island. Peter Schledermann

BOTTOM Woolen cloth of Norse origin is lifted out of the frozen ground of Skraeling Island by Peter Schledermann. K. McCullough

CHAPTER 2

The Strait of Anian

They came every year; first two, then three, then . . . many, a great many ships. —OOKIJOY NINOO TO EXPLORER CHARLES FRANCIS HALL, 1861

BY THE END of the fifteenth century, the icy waters and lands in the far north and the voyages of the Norsemen had become a dim memory, if remembered at all. Europe's interest lay farther south and in Asia. The riches of the Orient, particularly spices, had been carried overland to Europe since ancient times. Now, with the spread of Islam and the Moslem conquest of the Byzantine Empire, that route was closed to Christian Europe. This event inspired the Spanish crown to sponsor the search for a new route west across the Atlantic Ocean, proposed by an ardent Genoese navigator, Christopher Columbus.

In the aftermath of Columbus's voyage to the New World in 1492, both he and other navigators gradually mapped the great land masses of the Americas. Explorers by sea probed up and down the eastern shores of North America, seeking a passage through it to the riches of Cathay.

The quest for the Northwest Passage occupied the occasional attention of a number of nations, but the goal burnt most brightly for the English. Acting on the news of Columbus's discoveries, King Henry VII of England granted John Cabot and his sons Sebastian, Lewis and Sancius a patent to seek out new lands. Cabot's voyage in *Matthew* in 1497 was the first exploration of the New World under English colours. Between the northern tip of Newfoundland and Cape Breton Island, Cabot found traces of human settlement and immense schools of cod, which could be caught simply by dipping baskets into the sea. Cabot's push up the coast did not result in the discovery of a Northwest Passage, but it did open up a rich fishery that quickly attracted the attention of fishermen along the west coast of Europe. Cabot's son Sebastian picked up the quest and in 1508–9 may have reached Hudson Strait and the entrance to Hudson Bay, but he went no further north.

Other navigators, both Spanish and Portuguese, explored the coast of South America. But the first European glimpse of the western sea was from land, not the water. After trekking across the narrow Isthmus of Panama in 1513, Vasco Nuñez de Balboa sighted the Pacific from a Darien peak. If the land here was so narrow and close to the western sea, surely an ocean passage to it must exist somewhere on the coast. Spurred by Balboa's discovery, adventurers probed the South American coast for the oceanic passage to the west. Just eight years after Balboa became the first European to look west onto the Pacific, and within a few months of his conquest of the Aztecs, Hernán Cortés sent two expeditions to search the Mexican coast.

The only route that the Spaniards and their Portuguese rivals could find was to sail around the very tip of the southern continent. Ferdinand Magellan, tracing the South American coast, made his way round Cape Horn, entering the vast Pacific Ocean on November 20, 1520. While the Cape Horn route was occasionally braved by European rivals, starting with Francis Drake's daring entry into the Pacific in 1579, it was controlled by Spain. If other nations wanted to enjoy a sea route to the riches of the Orient, they would have to find another passage. The only direction that remained to search was north.

The next great voyages to map the coast of North America were in 1524–25, when Giovanni da Verrazzano and Esteban Gomez sailed all the way from Florida to Newfoundland, seeking a strait or waterway to Cathay. In 1576, the English soldier and adventurer Sir Humphrey Gilbert published *A Discourse for a Discoverie for a New Passage to Cathaia*. After arguing that a number of travellers' accounts, ancient authorites and a range of physical evidence proved the existence of a Northwest Passage, he noted: "It were the onely way for our princes, to possesse the wealthe of all the Easte parts (as they terme them) of the world, which is infinite."

The Voyages of Martin Frobisher, 1576–78

Sir Humphrey Gilbert's exhortations over the potential for great fortune excited interest in the English court and in business circles. They also supported the determination of one man—adventurer, pirate and master mariner Martin Frobisher. Gilbert had written his tract to generate support for Frobisher's grand ambition, to find a northerly sea route to Cathay. Frobisher was a product of his age, an Elizabethan sea dog willing to boldly push the limits.

Even as Gilbert penned his discourse, Frobisher had tenaciously gained an audience at court and political backing from the Earl of Warwick. Now he needed a licence from the powerful private concern that held, by royal charter, the exclusive right to explore to the north, northwest and northeast. These English mariners, who had commenced trading with Russia in 1533, opening a lucrative route to the White Sea, incorporated in 1555 as "The Company of Merchants Adventurers of England for the Discovery of Lands, Territories, Isles, Dominions, and Seignories Unknown," usually referred to as the Muscovy Company. The company wanted nothing to do with Frobisher, but Warwick and other influential backers prevailed.

Frobisher left Blackwall, England, on June 15, 1576, with thirty-seven men and three vessels: the 30-ton bark *Gabriel*, the 20-ton bark *Michael* and a small, 7-ton pinnace. Heavy gales dogged their progress, and the pinnace and its four-man crew were swallowed by the sea. On July 11, Greenland came into sight, but an attempt to land was defeated by the ice. "We had much adoe to get cleare of the yce by reason of the fogge," wrote Christopher Hall, *Gabriel*'s master. Feeling their way through more ice and fog, the two barks continued along the blocked coastline. Having had enough, and with an already damaged ship, the master of *Michael*, Gryffyn Owen, slipped away to England, leaving *Gabriel* and her eighteen-man complement alone. Frobisher was undaunted; the "worthy captain, notwithstanding these discomfortes, continued hys course towards the north-weast, knowing that the sea at length must needes have an endyng, and that some lands should have a beginning that way."

Frobisher's patience was rewarded on sighting the headlands of what he believed to be a strait, tending westward. Here, it seemed, was the entrance to the Northwest Passage. With a 30-mile-wide mouth, the "strait" reached far into the distance. Pushing into the strait on August 10, *Gabriel* explored what is now known as Frobisher Bay on Baffin Island. According to one contemporary account:

> And that land upon hys right hande, as hee sayled westward, he judged to bee the continente of Asia, and there to be devided from the firme of America, which lyeth uppon the lefte hande over-against the same. This place he named after his name Frobishers Streytes, lyke as Magellanus at the Southweaste end of the worle, havyng discovered the passage to the South Sea (where America is devided from the continente of that lande, which lyeth under the South Pole) and called the same straites Magellanes Streightes.

Some 120 miles into the strait, *Gabriel* entered a maze of small islands with narrow channels and shallow reefs between them. It was a dangerous spot, with strong currents interfering with the exhausting work of threading the ship through uncharted, unknown waters.

Landing on a small island deep inside his "strait," Frobisher climbed a hill and looked out on the sea. He "perceived a number of small things fleeting in the sea farre off, whyche hee syupposed to be Porposes, or Ceales, or some kind of strange fishe; but comming nearer he discouvered them to be men, in small boates made of leather." Contact was soon made with these people, the Baffin Island Inuit.

Frobisher and his men had a pleasant time for a few days, trading bells, knives, "looking glasses and other toyes" with the Inuit, who provided meat, fish, and seal and bearskin coats. The Inuit seemed familiar with iron and the ships, leading some modern scholars to speculate that they had seen Europeans before. Frobisher was also able to hire one of the Inuit men to serve as a pilot. But the easygoing relationship changed when the ship's boat, with five men, rowed the hired pilot ashore to a nearby village. The boat rounded a point of land and disappeared, never to be seen again.

With their only boat lost, Frobisher and his men could not reach land to conduct a search. After firing cannon and blowing trumpets to attract the attention of the missing sailors, they concluded the Inuit had seized the men. Inuit oral tradition insists that Frobisher abandoned the men, who stayed in the care of their hosts for two seasons and then sailed away. Robert McGhee suggests that the sailors, despite

Frobisher's command to not row out of sight, went ashore to trade on their own account or to seek the "charms of the Inuit women in the village." Having disobeyed an order from their captain, they stayed ashore too long, fearful of returning to punishment. Their mistake had tragic consequences.

Meanwhile, Frobisher, with a diminished, sickly crew barely able to work the ship, lured a man in his kayak close to the side of *Gabriel* with the promise of a bell. As the unsuspecting Inuk reached for the bell, Frobisher pulled him, kayak and all, onto the deck. With a captive as proof they had reached the Arctic, the English retreated. They also had their souvenirs of trade and various samples picked up from the island "in token of Christian possession." One of these tokens was a heavy black rock, "much lyke to a

"Frobisher's Straightes," as seen and mapped by the Elizabethans. Hakluyt Society

Sea dog, adventurer and pirate, the stolid Martin Frobisher was a favourite of his "Virgin Queen," Elizabeth. Born around 1540 in Yorkshire, Frobisher went to sea at a young age. He traded in Africa in defi- ance of Portugal's monop- oly there, occasionally, if the complaints were true, engaging in piracy. But Elizabeth and her govern- ment turned a blind eye to piracy when the victims were Spanish or Portuguese.

After his voyages in search of a Northwest Passage and the ill-fated gold-mining venture in Meta Incognita, Frobisher gained a knighthood for his actions in command of a ship engaging the Spanish Armada. Later, he joined the daredevil Francis Drake in a raid against the Spanish West Indies, but argued with his fellow sea dog. Frobisher died in 1594, fatally wounded in another action against the "Dons" of Spain.

Martin Frobisher stares boldly out from this portrait, painted before his third, failed expedition to Meta Incognita. The Bodleian Library, Oxford

seacole in coloure, which by the waight seemed to be some kinde of mettal or mynerall."

Arriving back in England on October 2, Frobisher presented his captive and the souvenirs he had collected as "sufficiente witnesse of the Captaines farre and tedious travell towardes the unknowne partes of the worlde." The unfortu-

nate captive soon died, but by then everyone's attention was distracted by some riveting news. The assayer who examined the black stone announced it was gold ore, "and that very ritchly for the quantity."

Swept away with gold fever, Frobisher and his backers quickly organized a second expedition, this time with Queen Elizabeth contributing £1,000 and a 223-ton galiass, *Ayde*. The two veterans of the first voyage, *Gabriel* and *Michael*, were fitted out for the return trip, and a force of 120 men, including soldiers and miners, was assembled. The expedition sailed from Blackwall on May 26, 1577. Reaching the "strait" on July 17,

An imagined scene of Frobisher's *Gabriel* anchored off Kodlunarn Island, 1576, with the ship's boat about to cast off. The five men and the boat disappeared, never to be seen again. Painting by Gordon Miller © 1995

Frobisher's men scoured the islands for more of the black ore. The rocky, snow-covered land made an impression, as did the discovery of a narwhal's carcass on a beach:

> On this west shoare we found a dead fishe floating, which had in his nose a horne streight and torquet, of length two yardes lacking two ynches, being broken in the top, where we might perceive it hollowe, into which some of our saylers putting spiders, they presently dyed. I saw not the tryall hereof, but it was reported unto me of a trueth; by the vertue whereof, we supposed it to be a sea unicorn.

Frobisher had his men erect a large pillar of rock, and in front of it he performed the ceremony for formally taking "possession" of the land. The blowing of trumpets at the ceremony attracted the attention of nearby Inuit, and a cautious trade resumed. The mood quickly soured, however, when the English decided to capture a man to serve as an interpreter. The Inuit gave fight, chasing Frobisher back to his boats and shooting him in the buttock with an arrow. The English rallied, capturing one man and hauling him off to their ships.

The situation turned even uglier a few days later when the English landed at an Inuit village and found European clothing they were sure had belonged to the sailors left behind the year before. Robert McGhee notes that this village was 120 miles away from the one where the boat had gone missing and that the clothing was probably more evidence of an existing trade between the Inuit and other Europeans. But Frobisher saw only evidence of kidnapping, and although he was guilty of the same offence, decided to attack the Inuit.

The battle was desperate. The Inuit fought with their wood and bone bows and lances while the English in their boats fought with firearms and arquebuses that shot steel-tipped arrows. When the English tried to land, the Inuit "resisted them manfullye . . . so long as their arrows and dartes lasted, & after gathering up those arrows which our men shot at them, yea, and plucking our arrowes out of their bodies, encountered afresh again, and maintained their cause, until both weapons and life utterly failed them." When the fight seemed lost, the Inuit jumped into the sea and drowned themselves rather than be captured. Six Inuit were killed, and three Englishmen were

Early engraving of the narwhal, or "sea unicorn," a fabled creature that amazed Frobisher's sailors. Vancouver Maritime Museum

injured. Frobisher named the spot Bloody Point "on occasion of the slaughter there."

Two women, one elderly, the other a young woman with a child, were captured. "The old wretch, who divers of our saylers supposed to be eyther a devil, or a witch," was stripped "to see if she were cloven footed, and for her oughly hew and deformity we let her go: the yong woman and the childe we brought away." With their captives in hand, the English continued up the "strait" and landed on an island they named Countess of Warwick's Island, known today as Kodlunarn (white man's island). After an attempt to find the five missing men from the first voyage met with no success, Frobisher turned his attention to mining "black ore."

The English fortified the island, as the Inuit kept trying to seize an English captive to ransom for their people. Any thought of seeking the Northwest Passage was put aside, as were Frobisher's instructions to establish a colony. The harsh climate prohibited it, in his estimation. In all, 158 tons of rock were mined and loaded on the ships. With winter setting in, the work was done quickly, some "having their belies broken" with hernias, and others "their legges made lame." By the third week of August, ice began congealing around the ships' hulls, and the expedition left for England. When the ships arrived home, the "ore" was amazingly found to be even richer than previously thought. On the basis of this assay, plans were laid for a third expedition.

Frobisher's third voyage, in 1578, was a mining venture, not a quest for the Northwest Passage. With fifteen ships and at least 397 men, it was, in the words of Robert McGhee, "the largest Arctic expedition ever mounted, before or since." The land they sailed to was now considered English soil, and "because that place & country, hathe never heretofore bin discouvered, and therefore had no speciall name, by which it might be called & known, hir Majestie named it very properly Meta Incognita [limits unknown], as a mark and nounds hitherto unknown."

The Inuit Remember Frobisher

In May 1861, Charles Francis Hall and his interpreter Tookoolito interviewed a female elder, Ookijoy Ninoo, about Martin Frobisher. She recounted a tale of three years of visits, first in two, then three, and finally in "a great many ships," saying that "five Inuits were killed by the *kodlunas*," and two women were taken away.

Ookijoy's account corroborated English reports of their encounters with the Inuit. She also told Hall of five men, captured by the Inuit, who stayed for one, perhaps more, winters. Then they built a large *oomien*, or ship, with a mast and sails, and left, but too early in the season; their hands froze, so they returned. When they recovered, they sailed away once more, and were never seen by the Inuit again. Ookijoy's tale solved the mystery of what had happened to the five men lost on Frobisher's first voyage.

Charles Francis Hall and "The discovery of Frobisher relics nearly three hundred years old, Sunday, August 11, 1861." From Hall, *Arctic Researches*

Frobisher's "Black Ore"

Martin Frobisher's second and third voyages resulted in a total of 1,404 tons of "black ore" being shipped back to England. When the rock was found to be worthless, it was used in a variety of building projects in Dartford, Kent, where blocks of it are still visible in some stone walls, particularly at the old Dartford Priory.

Working with samples of the rock from Dartford, from Ireland (where the wrecked *Emanuel* left her 100-ton cargo on the beach) and from Kodlunarn Island (the source), scientists D. D. Hogarth, P. W. Boreham and J. G. Mitchell concluded that the "ore" is actually a series of "metamorphosed and ultramafic rocks characterized by hornblende, unusual textures, an uncommon chemical composition (high iron and aluminum, significant chromium and nickel) and two ages (1470 and 1840 million years)." Their analysis confirms that the preliminary high gold and silver counts of Elizabethan times were due either to incompetence or deliberate fraud.

Model of Frobisher's fleet off Kodlunarn Island, 1578, loading ore as miners work on shore. Canadian Museum of Civilization/model by Steven Darby

The Inuit As the Elizabethans Saw Them

Dionyse Settle, who sailed with Martin Frobisher on the second voyage in 1577, described the Inuit they met:

"They are men of a large corporature, and good proportion: their colour is not unlike the Sunne burnt Countrey man."

"They weare their haire something long, and cut before either with stone or knife, very disorderly. Their women weare their haire long, and knit up with two loupes, shewing forth on either side of their faces."

"They apparell themselves in the skins of such beasts as they kill, sewed together with the sinewes of them. . . . They dresse their skinnes very soft and souple with the haire on. In cold weather or Winter they weare the furre side inward: and in Summer outward. Other apparell they have none but the said skinnes."

"They frank or keepe certaine dogs not much unlike Wolves, which they yoke togither, as we do oxen & horses, to a sled or traile: and so carrie their necessaries over the yce and snow from place to place. . . . And when those dogs are not apt for the same use: or when with hunger they are constrained for lacke of other victuals, they eate them: so that they are as needfull for them in respect of their bignesse, as our oxen are for us."

"They eate their meat all raw, both flesh, fish, and foule, or something per boyled with blood and a little water which they drinke. For lacke of water they will eate yce, that is hard frosen, as pleasantly as we will do Sugar Candie, or other Sugar."

The fleet sailed on May 31, 1578, laden with miners and soldiers, as well as supplies to build a small settlement. Reaching Arctic waters a little more than a month later, the ships encountered heavy ice and storms that plagued them for weeks. The "yce comming on us so fast," wrote Thomas Ellis, one of Frobisher's men, "we were in great danger, looking every houre for death." The bark *Dennis*, loaded with supplies, was battered into a leaky hulk and sank. As the ice continued pressing in, the sailors took down the topmasts and cut the anchor cables to hang over the sides as fenders. The men worked to ease the ships out of the ice, "some with capstan barres, some fending off with oares, some with plancks of two ynches thicke, which were broken immediatly with the force of the yce, some going out upon the yce to beare it off with their shoulders from the ships."

When the storm lifted, the ice retreated, but the ships were surrounded by a fog so thick "we scarce knew where we were." Frobisher, his bearings off, led the ships into a strait he thought was his goal, but after sailing up it for days, discovered they were in the wrong waters and retreated. Frobisher had mistakenly entered Hudson Strait. Finally, by the end of July, the fleet anchored off Kodlunarn Island and began mining.

Working strenuously for a month, the English loaded 1,300 tons of ore into their ships. The sea "was so much frosen and congealed in the night," wrote Ellis, "that in the morning we could scarce rowe our botes." Frobisher erected a small house on the island to see how it would fare during the winter and cached supplies. Presents were left behind, in the words of George Best, one of the company, "the better to allure those brutish and uncivill people to courtesie against other times of our comming." The fleet departed the waters of Frobisher's "strait" in early September. One ship, the bark *Emanuel*, was wrecked en route on the west coast of Ireland. The ship was beached and the 100 tons of ore aboard were landed. There it stayed, for new assays of the "black ore" showed that it was not gold at all, but worthless rock.

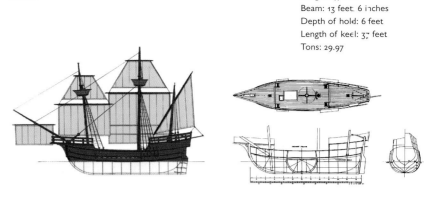

Gabriel

Length: 49 feet
Beam: 13 feet 6 inches
Depth of hold: 6 feet
Length of keel: 37 feet
Tons: 29.97

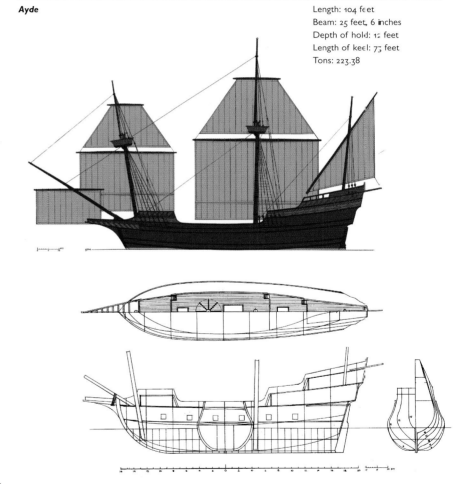

Ayde

Length: 104 feet
Beam: 25 feet 6 inches
Depth of hold: 12 feet
Length of keel: 73 feet
Tons: 223.38

Reconstructed profiles and plans for two of Frobisher's ships. Paintings/Drawings by Gordon Miller © 1999

In the aftermath of Frobisher's voyages, the site of his mines and Meta Incognita were lost to Europeans. Centuries later, many scholars believed that Frobisher had landed on Greenland's shores. However, Inuit on Kodlunarn Island pointed out surviving traces from Frobisher's expeditions to American explorer Charles Francis Hall in 1861–62. He also discovered a number of relics and traces of mining and building on Kodlunarn. Other explorers visited the island after Hall, digging and collecting "curiosities." Pioneering Arctic scholar Walter Kenyon was the first archaeologist to visit and study Kodlunarn in 1974.

In 1981, Donald Hogarth of the Smithsonian Institution, joined by other scholars, began a decade-long geological and archaeological investigation of the island. Hogarth's work gradually merged into a larger, co-operative project led by Dr. William Fitzhugh of the Smithsonian's National Museum of Natural History and Dr. Robert McGhee of the Canadian Museum of Civilization. Work continues to the present day under the direction of Dr. Reginald Auger of Laval University.

The Meta Incognita Project team has now excavated the remains of Martin Frobisher's camp and settlement from his expeditions of 1577 and 1578, offering the first archaeological evidence of European explorers in the Arctic. They have documented house sites, hearths, tent rings and mining trenches, as well as recovering a number of artifacts including iron ingots and ceramics, which amazingly survived centuries of souvenir hunters and the rigours of the Arctic environment. As part of the project, the Canadian and American teams also pursued archival research and gathered Inuit oral traditions, beginning with those transcribed by Hall and other explorers. The masterful work of the project team has provided the first comprehensive understanding of Frobisher's expeditions, of the first Arctic probe for the Northwest Passage and of the first recorded encounters between Europeans and Inuit.

There is even a suggestion, raised by Fitzhugh, that a pinnace full of Franklin's men may have been left behind at the end of the last expedition in 1578. If true, it would account for archaeological evidence that suggests smelting and ship-building or repair on Kodlunarn Island, and would modify our historical understanding, obtained from Inuit tales, about men left behind who built a boat and sailed off, only to be lost in the ice. Previous scholars, starting with Hall, believed that these were the men from the boat lost during Frobisher's first expedition. Frobisher, however, was convinced he had found some of their clothing in an Inuit camp, and that his men had been killed. That may be true, and the Inuit testimony may refer to another group of Frobisher's sailors, left behind in the haste to sail with the onset of winter at the end of the third and final voyage.

Inuit arrowhead, made from iron left behind by the Frobisher expeditions, discovered on Kodlunarn Island. Prince of Wales Northern Heritage Centre

Not a particle of gold had been smelted from the "promising" ore, and the finances of the company formed for the voyages were gone. The third expedition ended with many investors ruined, one promoter in prison, and Frobisher's reputation damaged.

John Davis Picks up the Trail, 1585–87

While the lure of gold had beckoned and temporarily shifted interest, the Northwest Passage was too valuable a prize to set aside for long. In 1585, a group of merchants led by William Sanderson of London sponsored a voyage in quest of the passage. The expedition, in the barks *Sunneshine* and *Mooneshine*, was led by John Davis, "a man very well grounded in the principles of the Arte of Navigation."

Sailing from Dartmouth on June 7, the ships were delayed by weather and did not reach Greenland until mid-July. After rounding Cape Farewell at the island's southern tip and heading northwest along the coast, landfall came at Godthab Fjord, where the explorers encountered a group of Inuit. After a cautious first day of observing each other, contact was made.

Leaving Greenland on August 1, the ships continued northwest, reaching Baffin Island on the sixth. Unaware they were in the same area where Frobisher had landed but recognizing some of the infamous "ore" in the cliffs, the Englishmen decided to land after spotting animals they first thought were goats or wolves:

> But when wee came neere the shore, wee found them to be white beares of a monstruous bignesse: we being desirious of fresh victual and the sport, began to assault them, and I being on land one of them came down the hill right against me; my piece was charged with haileshot and a bullet, tooke the water straight, making small account of his hurt. Then we followed him on our boate, and killed him with boare speares, and two more that night.

After a brief stay off Baffin Island's shores, sailing along the coast, Davis departed for home

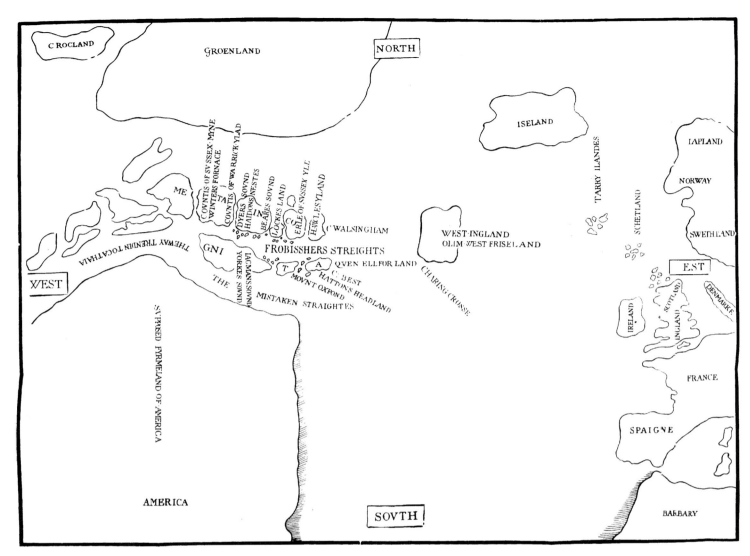

The world as seen by the Elizabethans after Frobisher's voyages. Hakluyt Society

at the end of August. His report to his patrons that "the north-west passage is a matter nothing doubtfull, but at any tyme almost to be passed" through seas "navigable, voyde of ayse, and the waters very depe" inspired a return expedition the following year.

Davis sailed from Dartmouth on May 7, 1586, this time with four vessels: *Sunneshine*, *Mooneshine*, the 120-ton *Mermayde* and a small 10-ton pinnace, *Northstarre*, which was carried broken down in *Mermayde*'s hold. Reaching Greenland on June 15, Davis found the shores choked with ice, so he continued west to Godthab Fjord, where he had stopped the year before. The Inuit kayaked out to the ships, and soon trade began while Davis's crew assembled *Northstarre* on the shore.

Davis's delight in his new friends notwithstanding, tension developed. The superstitious Elizabethans believed their Inuit hosts to be witches and that they had "many kind of inchantments, which they often used, but to small purpose, thankes be to God." After helping the English launch the pinnace, the Inuit invited Davis and his men to join in a ceremony by standing in the smoke of a smouldering fire. Davis thrust a nearby Inuk into the smoke and "willed one of my company to tread out the fire & spurne it into the sea, which was done to shew them that we did contemne their sorcery."

The Inuit, amazed by the large amount of iron used by the English, began to take some of this most valuable of materials from their guests. Davis reported they were "marveilous theevish," taking a spear, a sword, a boat, oars, cloth and anchor cable "with divers other things," including an anchor. The remonstrations of the English were met with a hail of stones, ending the friendly relationship. Davis used the pinnace to

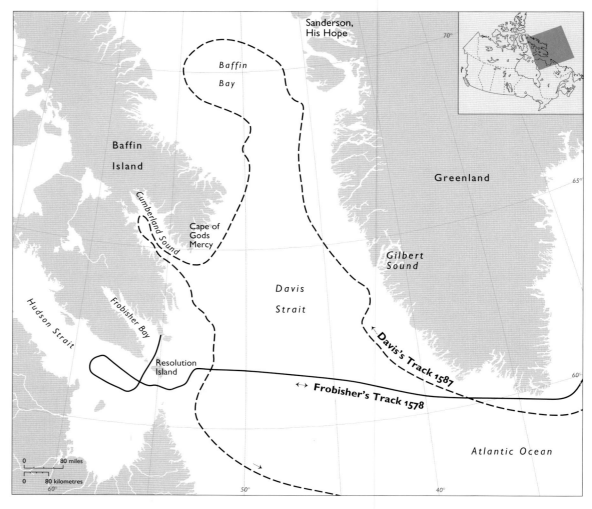

survey the nearby coast, but when he returned July 10, he was met by the officers and crews, who asked him to make a greater show of authority and force. Going ashore, Davis handed out bracelets as presents, but that evening, the Inuit attacked the ships with slings, hurling rocks against the hulls. "I changed my curtesie, and grew to hatred," Davis wrote. The English drove off the Inuit with gunfire, and the next day, when an attempt to commence trading was made, Davis seized an Inuk captive.

Weighing anchor, the expedition headed north, only to encounter heavy pack ice that slowed their progress while a thick, freezing fog clung to the ships, leaving ice on the decks and rigging. With his men grumbling, Davis retreated to Greenland, where he decided to split up the party, allowing the most unhappy of his officers and crew to return to England in *Mermayde*. He then continued west to Baffin Island in *Mooneshine*. After probing the island's east and

south coasts, he headed for the shores of Labrador. Always with an eye to commerce, Davis was delighted to discover rich schools of fish, which he set the men to catching.

But on September 6, the local Indians attacked a shore party that was loading the dried fish caught by the English the day before. Two of Davis's men were killed instantly and another two were "grievously wounded." Only the fifth and last man, with an arrow through his arm, managed to escape. As the wounded man was pulled onto the ship, a storm began to blow, and soon the crew was fighting to save *Mooneshine*. After five rough days, the storm abated, and Davis turned for home. In spite of the hardships, he reported that he had sold the sealskins obtained from the Inuit for a profit. These "furres" and the rich fishery he had found would pay the costs of another voyage.

On May 19, 1587, Davis left England with three ships, the two barks *Elizabeth* and *Sunneshine*, and the pinnace *Helene*. They were hit

by storms that damaged *Sunneshine* and *Helene*, delaying their progress. *Elizabeth* had to take the small pinnace in tow. Arriving off Greenland on June 16, the ships anchored and were soon greeted by the Inuit.

The crews landed the frames and planks of another pinnace, and the carpenters started assembling the new vessel. But relations between the Inuit and English deteriorated when *Sunneshine*'s master took "a very strong lusty yoong fellow" captive, possibly as an interpreter, but also probably as a "curiosity" for the people back home. The Inuit retaliated the next day: "The savages came to the island where our pinnace was built readie to bee launched, and tore the two upper strakes, and carried them away onely for the love of the yron in the boords." Flipping the boat on its side to use it as a shield against English arrows, the Inuit remained undaunted until Davis ordered a cannon to fire on them, although without the ball. When the Inuit retreated, carrying off the

planks from the pinnace, a crew from *Sunneshine* landed and took the now hopelessly damaged vessel back to the ships.

The English left on the first wind, separating into two parties. *Elizabeth* and *Helene*, with the damaged pinnace, headed west toward Labrador and its rich fishing grounds. Their orders were to fish and await the arrival of Davis in *Sunneshine*, who was to sail north along the eastern shore of Greenland, then pass through what is now known as Davis Strait and into Baffin Bay. *Sunneshine* reached as far north as 72°12', the site of today's Upernavik, before turning about and heading west.

Making landfall off the east coast of Baffin Island, Davis entered the broad waters of Cumberland Sound, which he had encountered on his first expedition. After probing the sound, he re-entered Davis Strait and worked his way down the coast, passing the entrance to Frobisher Bay, which he named Lumlies Inlet. The next day, a strong breeze carried *Sunneshine* further west, past

Frobisher Bay on Baffin Island runs 150 miles before terminating in a shallow shore. Corel

a "very greate gulfe, the water whirling and roaring as it were the meetings of tydes." This was
the entrance to Hudson Strait and the great bay
beyond it, soon to become the focus of a number
of expeditions seeking the Northwest Passage.

After reaching the spot he had selected for a
rendezvous with *Elizabeth* and *Helene*, Davis
searched in vain for them, finally sailing when it
became clear they had already left for home. After
Sunneshine reached England, Davis reported that
"with Gods great mercy" he had "sailed three-
score leagues further than my determination at
my departure. I have bene in 73 leagues, finding
the sea all open, and forty leagues between land
and land. The passage is most probable, the exe-
cution easie." Davis was on the right track; past
Davis Strait and Baffin Bay lay the entrance to the
Northwest Passage. But it would not be found
for centuries. The Little Ice Age still gripped the
Arctic, and the ice pack blocked further entry
past Davis's record push to 72° north latitude.

As well, other events intruded; England was
readying for war with Spain, and there was no
time to seek the Northwest Passage. The quest
was put off for a number of years.

The Mythical Strait

Meanwhile, on the Pacific coast of North
America, where Europeans imagined the western
entrance to the Northwest Passage lay, Spanish
explorers made no progress.

The accounts of several early voyages are
brief, including the 1542–43 expedition of Juan
Rodriguez Cabrillo and Bartolomé Ferrelo, the
1595 voyage of Sebastian Rodriguez Cermeño
and the 1602 expedition of Sebastian Vizcaino.
Each probed up the California coast between latitudes 32° and 42°, but no contemporary
accounts were published. Mapmakers still
penned speculative charts showing a wide strait
running through the continent. Named the Strait
of Anian, it cut through and passed by mythical
lands of great riches, some of them grand king-
doms like Quivira or the island of California,
populated by the Amazons and ruled by their
queen, Califia.

Spain's official policy of keeping its voyages of
exploration secret shrouded the north Pacific
coast in darkness and maintained the myth of the
Strait of Anian. The silence that surrounded
Spain's discoveries on the Pacific coast was filled
with wild tales that were eagerly seized upon.
One Lorenzo Ferrer Maldonado claimed that he
had sailed through the Strait of Anian, entering
the Pacific in 1588. The second account, amazingly enough, just may have been true. The story
came from a secretive explorer, a Greek-born
pilot named Apostolos Valerianos, or "Juan de
Fuca," as he was known to his Spanish employer.
Valerianos claimed that he pushed past the 42nd
parallel in 1592 and had sailed past a prominent
rock pillar into a "broad Inlet of Sea, betweene
47, and 48, degrees of Latitude" for twenty days,
encountering a land rich in gold, silver and other
precious items.

The supposed Strait of Juan de Fuca, thought
to be the Strait of Anian, remained on maps for
some time, although belief in its existence gradually fell out of favour. It was not until 1787 that
an American sea captain, Charles Barkley, sailing
up the north Pacific coast, entered a broad strait
in those latitudes that Spanish and British explorers, including James Cook, had missed. Cognizant
of the old tale, Barkley dubbed it the Strait of
Juan de Fuca, the name it bears to this day. Later

explorers conclusively proved that this body of water only separated Vancouver Island from the British Columbia mainland and was not the entrance to the Northwest Passage, but it took centuries for the myth of the Strait of Anian to die.

Failed Attempts

After England defeated the Spanish Armada, John Davis returned to the search for the Northwest Passage, but his principal supporter at court, Francis Walsingham, the queen's secretary, had died. In 1591, however, Davis joined the circumnavigation of the globe by Thomas Cavendish, who agreed that after reaching the Pacific, by way of the Straits of Magellan, Davis and his ship could head north up the Pacific coast of America to seek the western entrance to the passage. But Davis did not enter the Pacific; the voyage ended in failure, and his only achievement was the discovery of the Falkland Islands.

Another English seaman attempted to find the passage by sailing north in 1602. George Weymouth was sent out by the English East India Company in the ships *Discovery* and *Godspeed*, departing from Radcliffe on May 2. His instructions called for him to be away for at least one year as he searched for the passage. Following Davis's earlier track, Weymouth managed to push as far north as the 69th parallel, but fear of a mutinous crew caused him to retreat from the icy, fog-shrouded waters.

In 1606, the English East India Company decided to try again. John Knight, an "experienced Arctic navigator," was given command of the 40-ton bark *Hopewell*. Sailing from Gravesend on April 18, Knight reached the coast of Labrador on June 25. As they approached land, a heavy storm blew up, and ice, pushed by the storm, squeezed *Hopewell*, opening the bark's seams to the sea and tearing off the rudder. Knight managed to beach the sinking bark in a nearby cove. He and five of the crew rowed to a nearby island to reconnoitre the area, but Knight and three of the men never returned. The

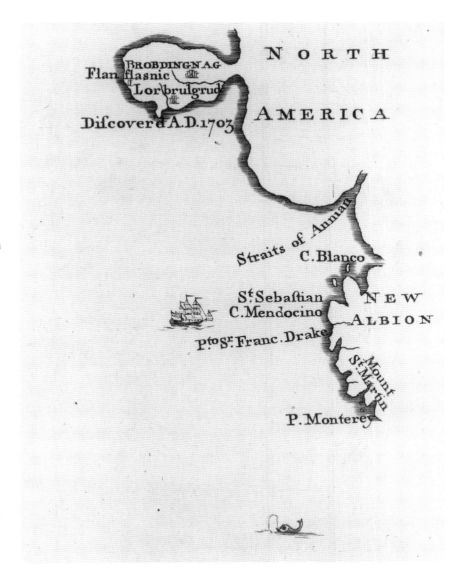

remaining crew beat back an Indian attack two days after Knight's disappearance. Manning *Hopewell*'s pumps, the sailors worked the bark to a nearby ice floe and tied up to it. Drifting with the ice, the ship reached Newfoundland, where the crew encountered a group of European fishermen. The crew and fishermen worked for nearly a month to repair *Hopewell*, and the battered bark arrived in England on September 24, the expedition a tragic failure.

These abortive ventures ended the search for a northward passage. The straits that Davis had described to the west of Baffin Island offered some possibilities, and it was there, to what is now known as Hudson Bay, that attention turned.

Fanciful eighteenth-century map of the Pacific coast of North America, showing the apocryphal Strait of Anian (here spelled Straits of Annian). Vancouver Maritime Museum/no number

CHAPTER 3

First Approaches

The bounds of America doth stretch many thousand miles: into the frozen partes whereof one Master Hutson an English Mariner did make the greatest discoverie of any Christian I knowe of, where he unfortunately died."
—CAPTAIN JOHN SMITH, 1616

WHILE THE VOYAGES of Martin Frobisher and John Davis had resulted in some hardship and loss of life, the drive into Hudson Bay introduced yet more suffering, tragedy and drama. But these efforts revealed what in time proved to be an even greater prize—Hudson Bay, the great inland sea that became the centre of a fur-trading empire spanning the continent. English merchants founded the Hudson's Bay Company, a fur-trading concern that became a commercial empire and played a major role in the exploration, settlement and development of Canada.

The Voyages of Henry Hudson, 1607–11

Henry Hudson was particularly interested in the "furious overfalls" that Davis had described. Here, Hudson reasoned, was the probable entrance to the Northwest Passage. It took him four years and four separate attempts to finally enter the "overfalls," the strait that now bears his name.

Hudson's first voyage began in May 1607, when he sailed from Gravesend, England, in the small sloop *Hopewell*. Chartered by the Muscovy Company to sail by way of the North Pole, which some argued lay in a warm, open, polar sea, Hudson instead encountered heavy storms, thick fog and ice off the coast of Spitsbergen (Svalbard), a group of islands in the Arctic Ocean. Pushing on, he finally stopped at 80°23' north—just 577 miles shy of the pole. It was a record for "farthest north" that would stand for 166 years. But records notwithstanding, Hudson found his way blocked. His return home was a meander to the west—biographer Donald Johnson thinks deliberately—in search of the Northwest Passage, until the threat of mutiny forced Hudson to return to England.

With the direct northerly approach blocked by ice, Hudson's next feint was to the northeast, across the top of Norway and Russia. Sailing again in *Hopewell* for the Muscovy Company, he cleared London on April 22, 1608, and headed for the River Ob, near the Arctic island of Nova Zembla. Many geographers thought the river was a direct route to Cathay. Reaching Nova Zembla in July, Hudson probed its shores, but ice thwarted a push to the mainland and the mouth of the Ob. "Void of hope of a Northeast Passage," Hudson wrote in his journal, "I therefore resolved to use all means I could to sail to the northwest." His destination was "that place called Lumley's Inlet [Frobisher Bay], and Captain John Davis's Furious Overfall [Hudson Strait], hoping to run there a hundred leagues into it, and to return as God should enable me." However, Hudson's crew threatened to mutiny, and on August 7 he turned the ship around and headed for London after providing "A certificate under my hand, of my free and willing return, without persuasion or force by any one or more of them."

Hudson's third voyage sailed under Dutch colours. Hired by the Dutch East India Company to push past Nova Zembla and into the Northeast Passage, Hudson sailed from Amsterdam on March 25, 1609, in the ship *Half Moon*. Pushing into the White Sea, Hudson quickly turned back in the face of heavy storms and headed—where else?—to the west. Discussions with his friend Captain John Smith led Hudson to investigate Smith's conviction that the entrance to the Northwest Passage lay immediately north of the new English colony of Jamestown in Virginia. Arriving off North America, Hudson surveyed the coast between Chesapeake and Penobscot Bays, entering promising inlets like the Hudson River only to find that they were not the elusive passage. He then shaped a course for England—a choice that surprised his Dutch employers and leads some historians to suggest that Hudson had actually remained in the employ of the Muscovy Company and simply made use of the Dutch.

The Last Voyage of Henry Hudson, painted by the Honourable John Collier, is the best known, yet imagined scene, from Hudson's final voyage. Tate Gallery, London

Hudson did not find a way through either the Northeast or Northwest Passages, but he did provide the Dutch with a claim to land in the New World. Of the various colonies the Dutch established in the aftermath of the voyage of *Half Moon*, perhaps the best known and most significant was Nieuw Amsterdam, which in time would become the City of New York.

Hudson's fourth and final voyage, according to his biographer Donald Johnson, finally received "official sanction to do what he had attempted three times before against the wishes of his employers and the will of his crew: search for the Northwest Passage." Hudson sailed from London on April 17, 1610, with a crew of twenty-two

men aboard the bark *Discovery*, previously used by Captain George Weymouth in his aborted attempt to seek the passage.

Fearing mutiny, which had cursed his three Arctic voyages, Hudson carried a man listed as a passenger, Henry Greene, to serve as his inform-ant among the crew. Reaching Greenland in early June, *Discovery* passed Frobisher's "strait" on June 9 and slowly tacked through ice. The bark did not enter Hudson Strait until the end of the month. Feeling his way through the ice-clogged strait, Hudson, according to passenger Abacuck Prickett, lost his resolve and called the crew together. Perhaps he feared an incipient mutiny. "Therefore he brought forth his chart and showed

Henry Hudson's ship *Discovery* working her way through the ice. From *The History of the Sea*

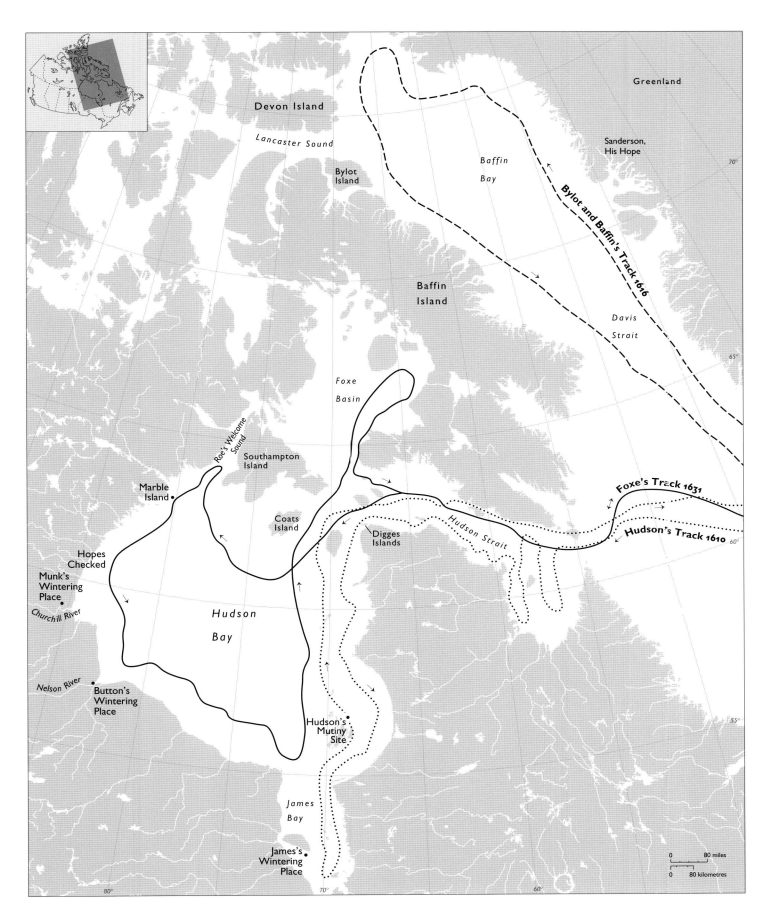

Greenland

Devon Island

Lancaster Sound

Bylot
Island

*Baffin
Bay*

Sanderson,
His Hope

70°

Bylot and Baffin's Track 1616

Baffin
Island

*Davis
Strait*

65°

*Foxe
Basin*

Roe's Welcome Sound

Southampton
Island

Marble
Island •

Coats
Island

Foxe's Track 1631

Digges
Islands

Hudson Strait

Hudson's Track 1610

Hopes
Checked

60°

Munk's
Wintering
Place •

Churchill River

Hudson

Bay

Nelson River • Button's
Wintering
Place

Hudson's
Mutiny
Site •

55°

*James
Bay*

James's
Wintering
Place •

| 0 | 80 miles |

| 0 | 80 kilometres |

80°   70°   60°

RIGHT **Ice on Hudson Bay.**
Mike Grandmaison

all his crew that he had entered the strait more than a hundred leagues farther than any other Englishman had and left it to their choice as to whether or not they would proceed any farther." While the crew, after some dissension, agreed to carry on, Hudson had essentially relinquished command.

Discovery made it through the strait in early August and found itself in "large sea," which was actually Hudson Bay. Hudson worked the ship south, along the eastern edge of the Ungava Peninsula. Finally, on November 1, at the end of James Bay, the southernmost shore of Hudson Bay, Hudson ordered the men to haul *Discovery* ashore and prepare for winter, "having spent three months in a labyrinth without end," noted Prickett. They had not found a passage after all, only a dead end.

Now trouble began in earnest. Disagreements and quarrels between the men, Hudson and his officers had marked the voyage since the beginning. Once in the bay, Hudson relieved his mate, Robert Juet, promoting Robert Bylot in his stead, and replaced the boatswain. He also had a falling out with the carpenter and the gunner, and even with his informant, Greene.

Discord grew throughout the winter, and Hudson compounded his problems by replacing Bylot, who had remained steadfastly loyal to the unpredictable, weak Hudson. Mutiny was close to the surface. When the ice retreated and

Henry Hudson

Nothing is known of Henry Hudson's early life; he burst onto the stage in middle age in 1607, already a seasoned a mariner, explorer and navigator when he first set out on an Arctic voyage. Presumably London-born, Hudson was married to a woman named Katherine, and had three sons. One of them, nineteen-year-old John, sailed with Hudson and presumably died with his father when they were

set adrift on Hudson Bay in June 1611.

Hudson's achievements, during the four years he sailed on his Arctic voyages of exploration, were many. He opened the Spitsbergen (Svalbard) whale fishery, charted a portion of the Northeast Passage, explored and charted the eastern seaboard of what is now the United States, and was the first explorer to enter and accurately chart the

straits leading to the bay that bears his name. It was in that bay that mutineers set adrift Hudson, his son and six of his crew in a small shallop. It would take other navigators on subsequent voyages to show that the promising body of water Hudson believed to be the entrance to the Northwest Passage was nothing more than a dead end.

Discovery broke out of James Bay on June 12, 1611, Hudson was seized, tied up and thrust into the ship's small shallop. With him went the "poor, sick lame men" and Hudson's son, John. They were given a gun, some powder and shot, the carpenter's tools, an iron pot and some pikes. Then the mutineers cast the shallop adrift and sailed away, leaving Hudson to fate.

Under the command of Greene, but with Bylot piloting, *Discovery* sailed out of Hudson Bay. Landing at Digges Islands to trade for food with the local Inuit, Greene and five men were attacked. Greene was killed and the others were mortally wounded, except for Prickett. En route to England, Juet died, and the remaining members of the crew, starving, put into Ireland. There, they pawned their anchor and cable for enough food to reach home. The mutineers destroyed much of Hudson's journal, no doubt because of incriminating remarks he had made about them, but saved his chart. This, and Bylot's report that the currents and tides of the bay indicated that it led to the Northwest Passage, saved the surviving mutineers from the gallows. It also inspired a return to Hudson Bay.

Into the Bay, 1612–15

Henry Hudson's discovery of the great bay diverted the quest for the Northwest Passage into its vast waters for over a century and a half. The first expedition to follow him left England in April 1612, when a group of English investors, newly incorporated as the "Company of the Merchants Discoverers of the North-West Passage" sponsored Captain Thomas Button to seek a passage west out of the bay. Button, in the ship *Resolution*, was joined by John Ingram, who commanded Hudson's bloodstained *Discovery*. He also took along Abacuck Prickett and Robert Bylot to show the way they had gone with Hudson.

Button entered Hudson Strait and stopped at Digges Islands, where he lost five men in a skirmish with Inuit after seizing two kayaks. Instead

---

Thomas Button

An Elizabethan sea dog like Martin Frobisher and John Davis, his predecessors in the Arctic, Thomas Button was from the parish of St. Lythans in Glamorganshire, Wales. After apprenticing at sea, Button may have served in Queen Elizabeth's navy during the time of the Spanish Armada in 1588. He later appears as captain of a royal pinnace, *Moon*, helping beat back a Spanish invasion of Ireland in 1601. Button was selected from the ranks of the navy to lead the Northwest Passage expedition of 1612.

Following his voyage to Hudson's Bay, Button returned to naval service and was knighted in 1616 for his role in suppressing Scottish rebellions the year before. Later, Button was rewarded with a promotion to rear admiral, and at the end of his career he served as Admiral of the Irish Coast. In the last years before his death in 1634, Button fought with his superiors over nonpayment of his salary and poor supplies, largely due to a corrupt naval establishment in power at the time.

---

of trying to find Hudson, Button headed west until he fetched up the shores of what is now the province of Manitoba, confirming that Hudson had sailed into a large bay. Reasoning that the Northwest Passage lay somewhere on the bay's western shore, Button scoured 600 miles of the coast between the Churchill and Nelson Rivers, but to no avail. He named the shore "Hopes Checked." With winter coming on, he moored his ships near the mouth of the Nelson River, hauling them up against the riverbank and surrounding them with a barricade of earth and logs for protection from the ice. The winter was hard, and many of his crew died of scurvy, including *Resolution*'s master, Robert Nelson. Button named the river for him.

When the ice retreated in April 1613, Button followed the coast north to a large sound that seemed to continue north between two bodies of land—the mainland and Southampton Island. He then returned to England to report that Hudson had found but a bay, though the tides offered hope that the Northwest Passage drained into it.

Button was followed in 1614 by William Gibbons, again in the old *Discovery*. Gibbons did not go far; heavy ice pushed the ship into a small bay on the coast of Labrador that the crew derisively dubbed "Gibbons His Hole." After a five-month stay, Gibbons worked the bark out of the ice as winter ended and headed home.

Gibbons's failure was regarded only as a temporary setback by the merchants who had sponsored him. These men, who had first employed

Hudson, then Button and finally Gibbons, did not waver in their resolve. They sent *Discovery* back, this time under the command of Robert Bylot. With William Baffin as pilot and navigator, Bylot made his third trip to the bay, sailing from England in April 1615. Entering the bay in late May, Bylot reconnoitred its northern end, reaching Salisbury Island in late June then heading farther north, along the shores of Southampton Island into the Foxe Basin. But ice and weather forced him to turn back. By September, he was home denouncing the idea that the "great bay of ice" was a route to the Orient.

Bylot and Baffin Probe North, 1616

Robert Bylot's backers were not done yet. If Hudson's strait and the bay were not the entrance to the Northwest Passage, then perhaps the other that strait Davis had charted, to the north, was the answer. Assembling a crew of fourteen, with Baffin along again as his pilot, Bylot sailed in *Discovery* from Gravesend on March 26, 1616. His instructions were to sail north to latitude 80° and then due west to Japan.

Discovery crossed the north Atlantic and pushed up through Davis Strait as Bylot hugged the Greenland coast. By the end of April, they stood off "Sanderson, His Hope," which was Davis's farthest north. From there, Bylot headed into parts known only to the Inuit and last seen by Viking mariners some three centuries past. Thick ice surrounded the bark as it pushed north to 77°45'—a farthest north that would not be surpassed for another 157 years.

During that wondrous summer, threading the ship through the ice, Bylot and Baffin mapped the shoreline of a large bay that was christened with Baffin's name. The Elizabethans marvelled at the summer cold: "Our shrouds, roapes and sailes were so frozen, that we could scarce handle them." Between Devon and Bylot Islands, they came to "another great sound," which Baffin named for his patron, Sir James Lancaster. "From here our hope of passage began to be lesse every day . . . for from this Sound to the Southward wee had a ledge of Ice between the Shoare and us." Though they did not realize it, they had just passed the entrance to the prize they sought. Two hundred and three years later, William Edward Parry of the Royal Navy would push through Lancaster Sound and enter the great maze of the Canadian Arctic archipelago that held the Northwest Passage.

Continuing on down the east coast of Baffin Island, *Discovery* crossed Davis Strait to reach the Greenland coast. After returning to England, Baffin reported that "there is no passage nor hope of passage in the north of Davis Straights. Wee having coasted all, or neere all the circumference thereof, and finde it to be no other than a great bay, as the voyage doth truely show." He was wrong, but no one pursued the passage north of Davis Strait for centuries. And, in time, with Baffin's map never published and the account of the voyage scarcely read, Bylot and Baffin's daring penetration of Baffin Bay was forgotten. The trail grew cold, and the quest for the Northwest Passage returned yet again to the waters of Hudson Bay.

William Baffin

Biographer Ernest S. Dodge describes William Baffin as "the most proficient navigator and observer of all the Arctic explorers of his period."

Born around 1584, Baffin's origins and early career are unclear. Like Henry Hudson, he came to the attention of history when first engaged in the exploration of the Arctic. Baffin sailed with Captain James Hall in 1612 to the east coast of Greenland, and on subsequent voyages as chief pilot for whalers working the waters off Spitsbergen. He then sailed with Robert Bylot on two voyages in search of the Northwest Passage, during which he accurately mapped portions of both Hudson and Baffin Bays.

After his Arctic voyages, Baffin joined the East India Company, sailing as master's mate in the ship *Anne Royal* to the Red Sea and Persian Gulf between 1617 and 1619. He returned to the Persian Gulf in the company's flagship *London* in 1620. Hostilities between England and Portugal over the region led to open warfare, and claimed Baffin's life in January 1622. While surveying the fortifications of Ormuz, Baffin was shot in the belly. "Wherewith he gave three great leaps, and died immediately," according to a witness.

Coats Island, in the north end of Hudson Bay. Corel

The Ordeal of Jens Munk, 1619–20

The King of Denmark and Norway, Christian IV, had been following the reports of England's sea dogs as they attacked the Arctic. Eager to secure the Northwest Passage for his own country, Christian commissioned an expedition in 1619. Jens Munk, a Norwegian-born subject of the Danish crown and a naval officer, was placed in command of two vessels, *Lamprey* and *Unicorn*. With a crew of sixty-four men, Munk sailed from Copenhagen on May 9, 1619, and raised the Greenland coast in late June. After an early July probe into Frobisher Bay, the ships entered Hudson Strait. The expedition's English pilot, John Watson, was familiar with the earlier voyages in search of the passage, so Munk sailed on

the track last pursued by Thomas Button, Bylot and Baffin into Hudson Bay.

But before entering the bay, Munk and his men had to contend with the ice. On July 13, the expedition's position "became perilous when the ice pressed us hard on all sides, making it impossible for us to either advance or retreat." The crews lashed *Lamprey* and *Unicorn* together, and

Munk let the ships drift with the ice. But the ice twisted *Unicorn* badly, dislodging part of the stem where it flared up to support the bowsprit. This "knee," as Munk termed it, was critical; if it tore loose, the entire bow would break up. The ship's carpenters were unable to move the heavy timber, but Munk managed to turn the ship around, so that the ice floe that had dislodged the knee in the first place now acted in the opposite direction to force the timber back into position.

With this disaster averted, Munk worked out of the ice and pushed on through the strait, stopping to trade with Inuit they encountered: "I . . . presented them with knives and all sort of iron goods. . . . After that, the natives gave me presents of everything they had, including different kinds of birds, and seal meat. All the natives embraced one of my men who had a swarthy complexion and black hair—they thought, no doubt, that he was one of their countrymen." Munk also replenished his supplies by hunting reindeer and named the harbour they stopped at Reindeer Sound.

Once back in the strait, however, the ships were again hemmed in by ice. When Munk put into another harbour, the ice came in with every tide, and the Danes had to work hard to keep it off the ships. The men, wrote Munk, "were completely exhausted" from the "incredible labour of pushing vast quantities of ice from the vessels or the incessant veering and hauling." Disaster threatened again when a large iceberg split apart. "Its collapse raised such huge waves that the *Lamprey* was almost put ashore. The sloop was fastened to the side of the *Unicorn* at the time, but we quickly got her clear of the ship. We lost one anchor, which was smashed against the bow of the *Unicorn* . . . but suffered no other damage."

Munk did not manage to work his way out of the strait and into the bay until August. Passing Digges and Mansel Islands, he headed southwest, crossing the bay for "three days and three nights." Winter was coming on, and in a storm of snow and hail, Munk anchored off the coast on

September 7, close to the mouth of the Churchill River. Within a few weeks, the crews shifted *Lamprey* and *Unicorn* to a more protected anchorage in a small cove just inside the river's mouth.

Scurvy, cold and disease ravaged Munk's crew, and his journal of that Arctic winter offers a stolid recounting of snow storms, starvation, ice opening up the hull of *Unicorn*, and then a progression of deaths.

By February 16, 1620, most of the crew, all quartered now on *Unicorn*, were "melancholy to listen to and miserable to behold," wrote Munk. As winter wore on, the dead, at first buried individually, were piled into common graves. But by mid-May, the dead were left in their bunks. At the end of the month, "there were only seven of us miserable people still alive, and we lay there day after day mournfully looking at each other, hoping that the snow would melt and the ice would drift away." Instead, more men died.

Jens Munk's map of his voyage into Hudson Bay.
Hakluyt Society

Only four men—Munk and three of his crew—remained alive by early June. Two of them were ashore, barely clinging to life. Munk and the sailmaker, meanwhile, held fast inside the ship. As his companion's life slipped away, Munk, surrounded by the stench of the dead and in deep despair, penned his last will and testament. Climbing out of his bunk and staggering on deck, Munk wrapped himself in as many clothes as he could find and lay down to die. In the morning he was still alive.

Then, on the shore, Munk saw the two men, whom he had thought were dead, walking across the ice to meet him. Helping Munk over the side of the ship, they slowly made their way over the ice pack to shore. The three built a fire and "later on we were able to crawl around looking for any green thing that grew out of the earth. Whenever we found something, we would dig it up and suck the juice out of its main root." Their health

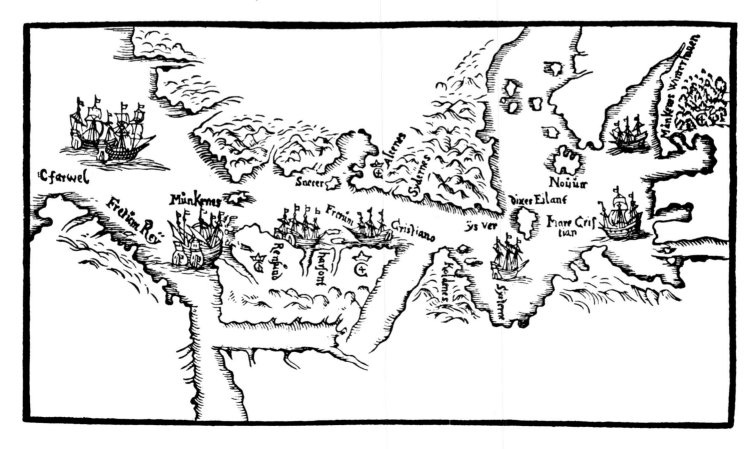

gradually returned, and by mid-June, when the ice retreated, they worked to ready the smaller *Lamprey* for the trip home.

On July 16, Munk and his two companions raised sail and left their winter harbour behind. Sailing through thick ice, they did not reach the strait until a month later. At last, on September 20, *Lamprey* put into the Norwegian port of Aldon, where Munk and his men burst into tears.

Christian IV ordered the exhausted Munk to return to the bay and continue Denmark's quest for the Northwest Passage, but even as the dutiful captain worked to assemble provisions and ready more ships, he was unable to man them. The horrific tales of the first voyage kept most potential explorers from volunteering, and the king had to abandon plans for a second voyage.

The next move was again England's, but their first new initiative was cursory and disappointing to the backers. William Hawkridge, with sponsorship from English merchants, re-entered Hudson Bay in July 1625. Very little is known of his course, except he appears to have kept to the northern part of the bay in waters already surveyed. His brief voyage, with nothing new added to the charts, ended after little more than a month in the bay.

Luke Foxe and Thomas James, 1631–32

Competition between two English cities—London and Bristol—inspired the next voyages to Hudson Bay in search of the Northwest Passage. London merchants petitioned King Charles I to grant a licence and a vessel for them to search for the passage. The king gave them the 70-ton pinnace *Charles*, commanded by Captain Luke Foxe. Bristol merchants, hearing this and fearing that London, should Foxe discover the passage, would secure exclusive rights to trade through it, petitioned for a ship and licence of their own. The answer was the 70-ton ship *Henrietta Maria*, commanded by Captain Thomas James.

Foxe sailed from Deptford on May 5, 1631, and by June 22 was off Hudson Strait. He followed its northern shore to reach the southern

coast of Southampton Island. He was now approaching the northwest corner of the bay, and between the island and the mainland, rediscovered the sound or strait that Button had probed in 1612–13. Foxe, fixing this as "Button's *ut ultra* [as beyond]," decided to tack south, after naming it "Sir Thomas Roes Welcome" (now Roes Welcome Sound) for one of his patrons.

Sailing on the reverse of Button's track, Foxe continued south along the shores of the bay, reaching Hopes Checked in early August. Farther south, he put into a small bay to assemble the ship's boat for closer surveying and to effect repairs to *Charles*. He soon discovered he was not the first to land there: "Wee found some store of Hogsheads and Pipestanes [barrels] , which had been yronbound, one Maine top, a top gallant Mast, diverse blocks . . . with divers reliques of some *English* vessell, which I tooke to have perished, or beene lefte not farre from hence; and Indeed I assure my selfe, it must be that of Sir *Thomas Button*." This was confirmed by the discovery of a board with the royal coat of arms from Button's time and a partial inscription left by Button showing "when and why he tooke Harbour with other expressions."

While searching for a tree to make a new mainyard for *Charles*, Foxe's men discovered more relics, including broken anchors, a cannon, "many round and crossbarre shot, or yron and lead," piles of rope, a fallen tent made of sails that covered a stack of firewood, and a large wooden cross. Before leaving, Foxe set up the cross again, with a lead tablet noting his visit and claiming the land "in right and possession, of my dread Soveraigne Charles the First."

On August 29, as *Charles* continued south along the bay's shore, Foxe fell in with Captain Thomas James's expedition, which had sailed to compete with him. Nonetheless, the two expeditions sailed together for the next three days, sharing supplies and comparing tales. Foxe was distressed to learn that although James was a skilled mathematician and navigator, "hee was no

Sea-man," and disparaged his ambitions: "I did not thinke much for his keeping out his flagg; for my ambition was more aetheriall, and my thoughts not so ayerie . . . to this was replide, that hee was going to the Emperour of Japon, with letters from his Majestie, and that if it were a ship of Majesties . . . hee could not strike his flag (keepe it up then quoth I) but you are out of the way to Japon, for this is not it."

When the expeditions parted company, Foxe left muskets and ammunition with James, who intended to winter on the bay, and continued south. A few days later, *Charles* reached a headland that Foxe realized was the entrance to the small bay where Hudson had perished. It was clear to Foxe that "all this undiscovered land, betwixt M. Hudsons & Sr. Thomas Buttons, was now perfectly finished by us . . . the further search of a passage, this way was hopelesse." Foxe decided to tack north and see if a passage lay there, "for I was not come to see what my predecessors had done, but to doe more."

Foxe did just that, heading past Digges Islands and up into the northern reaches of Hudson Bay. He charted the southwest shores of Baffin Island, not yet reached by any other expedition, and his farthest north in the bay, at 66°47', would not be reached again until 1741. Scurvy made its appearance, and with ice thickening and winter soon to come, Foxe decided to head for home. He argued with his critics that wintering with his weakened men might well have proved fatal for them all and that his return with the information he had gathered had been a greater service than disappearing in the far north.

James, in *Henrietta Maria*, had sailed from Bristol on May 3, 1631, two days before Foxe left London. Inexperienced and with a crew also unskilled in Arctic navigation, James did not enter the bay until mid-July and sailed southwest until he reached the vicinity of the Churchill River, where Munk had come to grief. Following the coast, James met up with Foxe close to the entrance to the lower bay.

When Foxe sailed on, James continued past the point and into the southern extremity, now known as James Bay, on September 2. Winter was coming, and a heavy storm lashed *Henrietta Maria*: "Our ship was so tormented and belaboured by seas washing over it from both sides and both ends that we were in most miserable distress in this unknown and lonely place." A week later, the ship was almost lost when she drifted into rocks while at anchor and pounded so heavily "that we saw some of our own planking drift by us." But *Henrietta Maria* held together, and the next morning, James took her out, though leaking, to "go to the bottom of Hudson Bay and see if I could find a way into the River of Canada."

In early October, James selected Charlton Island as his winter quarters. The crew unloaded *Henrietta Maria* and set up a camp that James named Charles Town. Thick slush was forming on the bay, and by November, "When we stood on the shore and looked towards the ship, she looked like a piece of ice that had been carved into the form of a ship." The slush around the ship was also freezing, and large ice floes constantly banged into the ship. At the end of November, James decided on a desperate course of action.

Rather than beach *Henrietta Maria* on the rocky shore, he decided to sink her in deep water, out of reach of the ice. The men worked to bore holes into her sides as *Henrietta Maria* pounded in the icy surf: "Nor would she sink as quickly as we would have liked." As the ship settled on the bottom, the men, with ice coating their beards and hair, stood by in the ship's boat and slowly rowed ashore through the slush, suspecting "that we had leapt out of the frying-pan into the fire."

James and his crew built cabins on the shore and settled in for a long winter, hunting and cutting timber for a new ship to occupy their time. Scurvy weakened the men, but in May, James found fresh sorrel to cure them. Work on the new boat was slow, and James decided to dig out the sunken *Henrietta Maria*. With iron bars, knives and hot water, the men chipped and hacked the cabins clear and dug down into the ice-filled decks. After a month's hard labour, the crew was rewarded by well-preserved provisions, including a barrel of beer, and the good news that the ship was still sound.

The sailors held a ceremony on the beach next to a large cross they had erected to mark the graves of four companions who had died that winter, then *Henrietta Maria* sailed on July 1, 1632. James paused briefly at nearby Danby Island, where he found a group of sharpened stakes that showed signs of being worked by iron tools, giving rise to the suspicion that the tiny island was the site of Henry Hudson's final camp after being set adrift by his mutinous crew. *Henrietta Maria* cleared James Bay and followed the previous year's track, crossing the bay and heading for Hudson Strait. James, like Foxe before him, pushed north past Southampton Island and into Foxe Basin. But the threat of another winter and the appearance of ice alarmed the crew, and James turned for home.

James concluded, correctly, that a number of tales about the passage were "absurd" and that fanciful maps showing the Strait of Anian near Hudson Bay were "mere fabrications." However, he noted, "One thing . . . is certain. The northern parts of America, to the lattitude of 80 degrees and upwards, have been discovered only through the industry of our own nation. And this has been so carefully done, through the labours of several different men, that the supposed passage must lie to the north of 66 degrees, for south of that the mainland has all been explored. North of 66 degrees, however, is a region of extreme cold, pestered with ice and other hazards." If the Northwest Passage existed, it would be "quite narrow in several places," choked with ice and ultimately of no value, for easier, though longer, routes existed around Africa. He concluded: "There are certainly no commercial

Likeness of Thomas James, whose voyage to Hudson Bay nearly ended in disaster.
Hakluyt Society

Rime of the Ancient Mariner

A number of scholars have suggested that Samuel Coleridge drew some of the inspiration for his famous poem *Rime of the Ancient Mariner* from *The Strange and Dangerous Voyage of Captain Thomas James*, James's account of his near-fatal expedition to Hudson Bay. While the issue is still debated, Coleridge's account of a frozen journey has images that appear to be drawn from the words of someone who had been there, perhaps the articulate and literate James:

And now there came both mist and snow,
And it grew wondrous cold;
And ice, mast-high, came floating by,
As green as emerald.

And through the drifts the snowy clifts
Did send a dismal sheen:
Nor shapes of men nor beasts we ken—
The ice was all between.

The ice was here, the ice was there,
The ice was all around:
It cracked and growled, and roared and howled.
Like noises in a swound!

Ring dial, seventeenth or eighteenth century. An instrument used to determine latitude. Vancouver Maritime Museum

benefits to be obtained in any of the places I visited during this voyage."

The Fur Traders Arrive

After James and Foxe, no European vessel visited Hudson Bay until 1668, when the 40-ton *Nonsuch* arrived to establish a fur-trading outpost at the extremity of James Bay. That outpost, Rupert House, was the beginning of the greatest commercial enterprises in North America, the fur-trading empire of the Hudson's Bay Company (HBC). The investors in *Nonsuch*'s voyage were

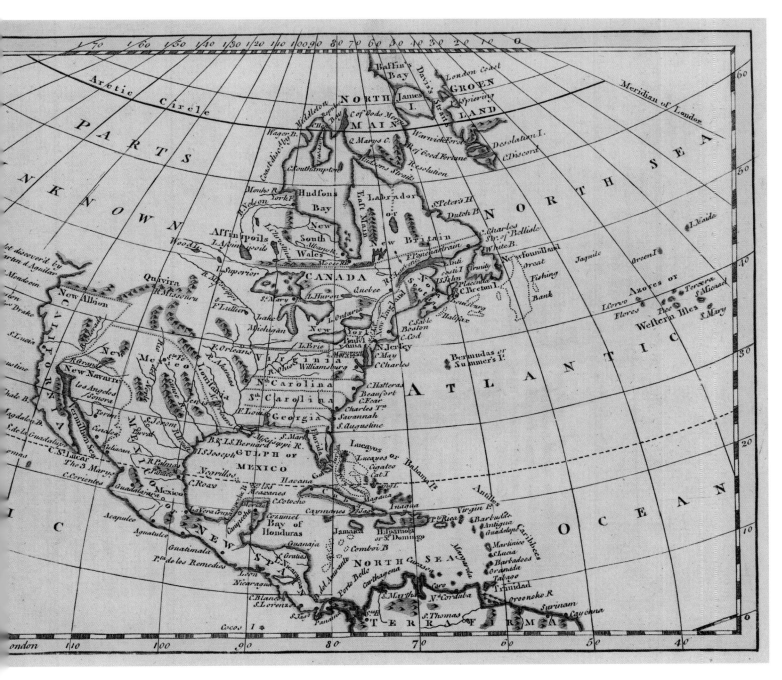

chartered, with a licence from King Charles II, as the "Company of Adventurers Trading into Hudson's Bay." Using Hudson Bay as the centre of activities, its annual supply ships arriving with trade goods and leaving with furs, the Company established a solid foothold.

The Hudson's Bay Company was not, however, interested in the quest for the Northwest Passage. Its first decades on the bay were filled with the struggle to establish trade, build forts and outposts and, after 1689, to survive continual battles with the French. The English lost their outposts on the bay to the French, but regained them with the peace and the Treaty of Utrecht in 1713. The man the Hudson's Bay Company sent to re-establish trade, James Knight, was a veteran trader with a strong desire to find both the Strait of Anian and the great riches that he believed lay in the north.

After gathering accounts of "yellow mettle" and "several ships in the Western Seas which I cannot think to be Spaniards . . . I rather take them to be Tartars or Jappannees vessels," Knight persuaded his employers to grant him two ships

Map showing Hudson Bay, as the world knew it after Middleton's voyage of 1741–42. Vancouver Maritime Museum to seek both the passage and the gold. In June 1719, he sailed from England with a crew of thirty-seven men in the 100-ton *Albany* and the 40-ton *Discovery*. Reaching the western shores of Hudson Bay, Knight established a settlement on Marble Island, close to Chesterfield Inlet, which he believed to be the opening of the "streights." Instead, he and his men were trapped by an early winter and thick ice. They were never heard from again.

In 1722, the Hudson's Bay Company ship *Whalebone*, passing by Marble Island, landed and discovered the ruins of a house built by Knight's expedition, a medicine chest, ice poles and parts of a ship's mast, but no trace of the men. In 1767, the HBC ship *Success* also landed on the island and discovered the by then forgotten site of Knight's tragedy. Returning the following year, the HBC men dug up graves on the island and questioned the local Inuit, who reported that some of Knight's men had survived to at least 1720. The last two survivors "frequently went to the top of an adjacent rock and earnestly looked to the South and east, as if in expectation of some vessels coming to their relief. After continuing there a considerable time together, and, nothing appearing in sight, they sat down close together, and wept bitterly. At length one of the two died, and the other's strength was so far exhausted, that he fell down and died also, in attempting to dig a grave for his companion."

Christopher Middleton and William Moor, 1741–47

In 1741–42, the British Admiralty, acting on the constant lobbying of politician Arthur Dobbs, sent two expeditions into Hudson Bay to renew the quest for the Northwest Passage. Dobbs, a critic of the HBC, felt that while they slept at the edge of a frozen sea, the French, with their presence in Canada, might discover the long-sought passage. Captain Christopher Middleton, a former HBC officer, was placed in command of the first expedition and of the ship *Furnace*; he was joined by William Moor, in *Discovery*. Sailing from London on June 8, 1741, the ships reached the bay late in the season, and Middleton decided to winter at the HBC post at the mouth of the Churchill River. It was a fatal decision for ten of the crew, who died of scurvy.

On July 1, 1742, the expedition resumed. *Furnace* and *Discovery* headed north, touching at Rankine Inlet and sailing up past "Sir Thomas Roes Welcome," which turned out to be a narrow strait between Southampton Island and the mainland. A large body of water, opening to the northwest, was partially surveyed and named Wager Bay. The ships then continued north, past Cape Hope and into Repulse Bay. Middleton had reached the edge of the Arctic Circle, going almost as far north on the western shore of Hudson Bay as Foxe had. But at the bay he named, appropriately, Repulse, the intervening land closed in and he retreated. Tacking back to the tip of Southampton Island, Middleton was able to see a large "Frozen Strait" that lay

---

The Hudson's Bay Company

The dazzling potential for profits from the North American fur trade inspired the creation of one of the largest and most powerful business concerns on the continent, the Hudson's Bay Company (HBC).

Chartered in 1670 by King Charles II as the "Company of Adventurers of England Trading into Hudson's Bay," it was granted authority to exploit the resources of a large part of the continent—4 000 000 square kilometres (1.5 million square miles)—including the shores of Hudson Bay, the Arctic and 40 per cent what eventually would become Canada, as well as part of the northern United States.

The Hudson's Bay Company not only controlled a vast territory, it also had the power to make and enforce laws, build forts, and maintain military forces to protect its trade. The Company employed a fleet of its own, including ships that annually sailed into Hudson Bay with supplies and trade goods, then returned to England laden with furs. In its occasional forays in search of the Northwest Passage, the HBC used its ships as well as its land-based traders and voyageurs. The greatest role the HBC played in the quest, however, came near the end of the search for the passage in the first half of the nineteenth century.

between the island and the Melville Peninsula. It was, as he named it, clogged with ice and impassable. With scurvy affecting his crews, Middleton decided to head back to England.

Middleton's voyage clearly indicated that a northern route out of Hudson Bay and farther north was impossible. Dobbs, however, refused to believe it and bitterly attacked Middleton. He was joined by some of Middleton's disgruntled crew, who claimed that Wager Bay was actually the long-sought strait and Middleton was concealing the fact. In the ensuing controversy, Middleton's reputation was ruined.

Parliament spurred the quest in 1744 by passing an Act promising a reward of £20,000 "to any of His Majesty's subjects" who should sail between "Hudson's Bay and the western and southern ocean of America."

Arthur Dobbs selected Middleton's former officer, William Moor, to head a second expedition. Moor sailed, with private backing, in the ships *Dobbs Galley* and *California* in May 1746. Reaching the bay in August, he decided to winter at York fort. Like Middleton, he suffered a severe winter, and seven of his men died.

Resuming his voyage in June 1747, Moor sailed north along Middleton's old course. His only variation from his old commander's track was when he entered Chesterfield Inlet, which trended to the northwest, and when he pushed farther up Wager Bay to its end. "Our hitherto imagined strait," he wrote, "ended in two small unnavigable rivers." Moor retreated home in late August, his crew ill with scurvy.

Dobbs now ended his quest, but not his attacks on the Hudson's Bay Company, which, he felt, controlled the bay to the detriment of other British enterprise in the region. The HBC, for its part, pursued the examination of the bay's coast, sending expeditions to probe every inlet and river. These forays culminated in 1761–62, when William Christopher searched Chesterfield Inlet in the sloop *Churchill*. His voyage raised hopes that the inlet might just be the Northwest

---

An Archaeological Encounter with Knight

Archaeological investigations by Owen Beattie between 1989 and 1991 at Marble Island disclosed traces of the settlement where James Knight and his men had wintered. This included the foundation of the house that they built and a number of artifacts, including buttons, shoes and a single, tobacco-stained human tooth—but no traces of the graves or human remains rumoured to be on the island. Beattie theorizes that Knight took his men and escaped from the island to find an unknown fate in another area. Knight's two ships were not used in the escape, however. The submerged hulks of *Albany* and *Discovery* were pinpointed by Beattie and were subsequently identified in 1994 by a Parks Canada diving expedition led by Robert Grenier. They are the earliest discovered wrecks of Arctic exploration vessels.

Both ships had been stripped of their fittings, rigging and upper works, including the decks. Heavy rocks had been used in an apparent effort to sink them, perhaps below the ice where they would be safe during the winter. Future examination of the wrecks may provide more evidence of how and perhaps who, stripped the ships—and perhaps an explanation for why two seemingly sound vessels—the only way home—were partially dismantled and sunk. For now, however, archaeology has posed new questions, and as yet few answers, to the centuries-old mystery of the lost Knight expedition.

Passage, but on his return the following year, that inlet too was found to be another dead end.

The 162-year exploration of Hudson Bay in search of a Northwest Passage had consistently proven to be just that—a dead end. Thomas James was correct in asserting that the future lay far north, "pestered with ice" and fraught with peril.

Ice all over

Sea Horse Point

Icy Sea

70

Serz Kamen

Straits

Bearings

Prince of Wales Cape

sledge I.

Norton Bay

Route I.

St Lawrence Isle

Here the water was shole we Land to get nearer the Land

Bird I

Cape Newingham

60

CHAPTER 4

British Endeavours

*Who are you? what are you? where do you come from?
Is it the sun or the moon?* —GREENLAND INUIT TO JOHN
ROSS'S EXPEDITION, 1818

ON JULY 18, 1771, Samuel Hearne, a
Hudson's Bay Company fur trader,
stood on the shores of an ice-choked
sea and gazed north. He was looking
out at the waters of the fabled Northwest Passage,
195 years after Martin Frobisher first set out to
find it. But Hearne did not know this was a stretch
of the elusive passage. He had followed the course
of the Coppermine River north to its mouth, on
foot and by boat with a Chippewa Indian guide,
Matonabbee, in search of copper mines and open
waters that might be the polar sea.

Standing on the shore, Hearne saw open
patches of water that marked where the land
came into contact with the ice. "The sea is full of
islands and shoals, as far as I could see," he wrote.
"I erected a mark, and took possession of the
coast." Hearne was the first European to reach
the North American shores of the Arctic Ocean,
although he noted, resignedly, that "my discoveries are not likely to prove of any material advantage to the Nation at large."

Two years later, Britain sent an expedition,
this time by ship, in search of the polar sea.
Commanded by Captain Constantine Phipps, the
ships *Racehorse* and *Carcass* sailed between
Greenland and Svalbard, bound for the North
Pole in June 1773. Many scientists believed that
after working through a fringe of ice, Phipps's
ships would enter an open polar sea. The thick
ice halted him at 80°43' north, but his observations of the icy sea were important and gave the
Admiralty food for thought.

The next Englishman to glimpse the polar sea
was James Cook. On his third and final voyage,
Cook pushed north, along the Pacific coast of
North America, arriving at the Bering Strait in
November 1778. Sailing in the wake of Vitus
Bering, who had discovered the strait in 1728,
Cook's ships *Resolution* and *Discovery* continued
farther north, reaching 70°, on the edge of the
Chukchi Sea. Stopped by a solid barrier of ice,
Cook named the nearest landfall Icy Cape as he
retreated. Only later would it be ascertained that
he had actually entered the western end of the
Northwest Passage. But Cook never knew, for
he sailed on to meet his death in the Hawaiian
Islands.

FACING PAGE Britain's first
penetration of Bering Strait.
This pencil-and-ink chart,
kept aboard Captain James
Cook's ship *Resolution* in
August 1778, shows the ship's
track and the shoreline of
Bering Strait leading into the
Arctic. The original chart,
drawn by William Bayley, has
notations made by Cook's
officers, including William
Bligh. Vancouver Maritime
Museum

RIGHT Samuel Hearne's
name carved into a rock at
Sloop Cove, near Churchill,
Manitoba. Hector Williams

A

JOURNEY

FROM

Prince of Wales's Fort in Hudson's Bay,

TO

THE NORTHERN OCEAN.

UNDERTAKEN
BY ORDER OF THE HUDSON's BAY COMPANY,
FOR THE DISCOVERY
OF COPPER MINES, A NORTH WEST PASSAGE, &c.
In the Years 1769, 1770, 1771, & 1772.

By SAMUEL HEARNE.

LONDON:
Printed for A. STRAHAN and T. CADELL:
And Sold by T. CADELL Jun. and W. DAVIES, (Succeſſors to
Mr. CADELL,) in the Strand.
1795.

**The title page of Samuel
Hearne's book, *A Journey . . .
to the Northern Ocean.***
Vancouver Maritime Museum

In 1789, Alexander Mackenzie, another Hudson's Bay Company fur trader and explorer, left Fort Chipewyan, at the junction of the Peace and Slave Rivers. He travelled by birchbark canoe, searching for a great river which, according to Indian accounts, flowed into the sea. Mackenzie hoped this sea might be the Pacific. On June 29, with the help of a Copper Indian guide, he entered the great river. Two weeks later, he reached the mouth of the river, at the head of a huge delta. After taking his bearings, Mackenzie realized that he had reached the Arctic Ocean, not the Pacific. He returned south on what he is said to have called the River of Disappointment. On his 102-day trip, he covered 3,000 miles. Like Hearne, Mackenzie did not think much of his discoveries, but his journey down the river, now named for him, opened up the region to later fur traders and explorers.

Mackenzie's next journey saw him head west, this time successfully reaching the shores of the Pacific in July 1793, narrowly missing the arrival of HMS *Discovery* and *Chatham*, under the command of George Vancouver. Vancouver, a midshipman on Cook's final voyage, had been sent, among other things, to scour the portions of the Pacific Northwest Coast not surveyed by Cook. His voyages of between 1791 and 1795, at times in consort with Spanish expeditions also seeking the western entrance to the passage, meticulously charted the coast. Numerous inlets penetrated the coastline, but they all ended in narrow, high canyons that gradually drew closed. Vancouver's voyages conclusively ended speculation about the existence of an entrance to the Northwest Passage along the Pacific coast south of the Bering Strait. He noted that his expedition had "truly determined the non-existence of any water communication between this and the opposite side of America within the bounds of our investigation, beyond all doubts and disputance."

Exploration, which for the last few decades had occupied the great powers of Europe, came to a halt during the wars with Revolutionary and Napoleonic France. And, just as those wars came to an end, conflict with the young United States kept Britain from returning to exploration.

The Quest Renewed, 1818

Reports of retreating ice in Baffin Bay in 1815, 1816 and 1817 drew the Admiralty's attention, particularly when whaling captains with years of experience, like William Scoresby, Jr., wrote: "I observed on my last voyage (1817) about two thousand square leagues [18,000 square miles] of the surface of the Greenland seas . . . perfectly devoid of ice." Since the arrival of the Little Ice Age a few centuries before, a "vast barrier of ice" had blocked ships from entering the high Arctic. Now the barrier was gone, and the route to a Northwest Passage was seemingly open.

In 1818, John Barrow, Secretary of the Admiralty, revived Britain's search for the Northwest Passage. After gathering as much information as he could from the accounts of earlier explorers, he concluded that the currents running out of Davis Strait, Hudson Strait and along the coast of Spitsbergen showed that "the water supplied through the Strait of Behring . . . into the Polar Sea, was discharged, by some opening, or other, yet to be discovered, into the Atlantic."

Barrow's plan was approved by the British government, in part motivated by the concern that a foreign power might "discover" the passage. This Royal Navy expedition, in 1818, saw four ships set out to explore the Arctic, sailing up the east and west coasts of Greenland. David Buchan, commanding HMS *Dorothea*, and John Franklin, commanding HMS *Trent*, took the east coast, heading toward Spitsbergen and the North Pole. John Ross in HMS *Isabella* and W. Edward Parry in HMS *Alexander* took the west coast. Ross's instructions were simple: "to find a passage, by sea, between the Atlantic and Pacific . . . by way of Davis' Strait."

Buchan and Franklin were stopped by ice off the coast of Spitsbergen. Ross also failed, spectacularly, by heading up Lancaster Sound, and then turning back. He claimed that as he had pushed west into Lancaster, the skies had cleared: "I distinctly saw the land round the bottom of the bay, forming a chain of mountains. . . . The mountains . . . were named Croker's . . . after the Secretary to the Admiralty." Ross's officers later swore that he alone had seen the mountains and that some of them had privately questioned the order to retreat. But Ross was "perfectly satisfied that there was no passage in this direction."

It was the worst mistake of Ross's career. The shaded line he drew on his charts haunted him to the end of his life. "Croker's Mountains" overshadowed his achievements on the voyage, which included the first survey of Baffin Bay in centuries, the pioneering use of a deep-sea clamshell

---

Isabella

The 382-ton *Isabella* was built at Beverly, England, for part-owner Captain Heselwood of Hull. She was 110 feet long with a 28-foot beam. In January 1818, after hiring *Isabella*, the Admiralty strengthened and outfitted her at the Royal Navy yard in Deptford for John Ross's Arctic expedition. Ross selected *Isabella* as his flagship.

After the expedition returned to England, *Isabella* was handed back to her owners and traded between Canadian ports and Hull, England, until the early 1820s. By 1825, she was back in the Arctic, working as a whaler. Two years later, *Isabella* reported a very profitable season, with twenty-three whales killed and 250 tons of oil rendered under the command of Richard Wallis Humphrey of Hull. Another good season in 1832 saw *Isabella* return to Hull with 275 tons of oil. But the crowning glory came the following year, in 1833,

when Humphrey and *Isabella*'s crew rescued the ship's former commander, John Ross, and his missing Arctic expedition.

Isabella's career came to an end in Arctic waters on May 12, 1835. Under the command of Captain Robert Carlill, the ship was lost in thick weather off the Whale Fish Islands. The crew suffered badly from frostbite before rescue. *Isabella* was one of five Hull-based Arctic whalers lost that year.

Landing the Treasures, or Results of the Polar Expedition !!!

Cartoon lampooning John Ross's expedition to Baffin Bay, 1818. Mineral samples, a polar bear and an erstwhile Inuk parade behind Ross. The men are all missing their noses, ostensibly from losing them due to the Inuit style of greeting by rubbing noses.
Scott Polar Research Institute, Cambridge

dredge to collect samples, and the Royal Navy's first encounter with native Inuit of the region, who had never before seen white men. But all of this was ridiculed and angrily swept aside by Barrow, who called Ross's description of mountains blocking his way "a pitiable excuse for running away home."

Barrow absolved Ross's junior officers of blame, particularly W. Edward Parry, the bright, energetic, twenty-eight-year-old lieutenant who had commanded *Alexander*. Barrow noted with interest an anonymous report that "every officer and man," other than Ross, had "made up his mind that *this must be the north-west passage*."

Edward Parry's First Voyage, 1819–20

John Barrow had no qualms in selecting Edward Parry as commander of the next Arctic expedition. The Admiralty gave Parry HMS *Hecla*, a for-

mer "bomb," or shore bombardment vessel, and HMS *Griper*, an 180-ton brig under Lieutenant Matthew Liddon's command. *Hecla* was a good choice. "Bombs" were bluff, stout vessels built to withstand the shock of heavy mortars being fired from their hulls. Reinforced with double planking and a thicker bow, *Hecla*, Parry noted, "will combine everything we want—*great* strength, capacity of hold, good sailing, and fine accommodations for Officers and Men."

Griper was another matter. Too small, her sides had been raised, making the brig prone to capsize. Extra ballast helped stabilize the hull, but at the expense of some of her stores, which were passed on to the already fully laden *Hecla*. Parry fumed that "these paltry Gunbrigs are utterly unfit for this service!"

Hecla and *Griper* sailed from England on May 11, 1819. Parry's orders were to proceed to

W. Edward Parry

Born at Bath, England, in 1790, William Edward Parry joined the Royal Navy at age thirteen, taking part in the last years of the Napoleonic Wars and the war against the United States. In 1817, he volunteered to join an expedition to the Congo, but after reading a newspaper report on the proposed expedition to seek the Northwest Passage, he wrote to a family friend that he was "ready for hot or cold."

Secretary of the Admiralty John Barrow was impressed by Parry and ensured that the young but experienced lieutenant was appointed to John Ross's Arctic expedition, launching him on a decades-long career in the north. Parry became one of the Royal Navy's most experienced Arctic navigators and explorers. Through a combination of luck, skill and determination, he penetrated farther into the Northwest Passage in 1819–1820 than any other explorer would for more than thirty years. And on his failed attempt to reach the North Pole in 1827, Parry's "farthest north" of 82°43'32" stood as the record for decades.

Captain Parry was knighted in 1829, having served simultaneously both in the Arctic and as the Royal Navy's hydrographer. When his first wife, Isabella Stanley, died, Parry married Catherine Hoare in 1841 and fathered thirteen children. Promoted to rear admiral in 1853, Parry's last post was as lieutenant governor of the Greenwich hospital for naval pensioners.

Parry's expeditions captured popular attention and the acclaim of his peers. Tall, handsome, intelligent and resolute, he was an imposing figure. His boldness as an explorer was tempered by his skills as an administrator and leader. Concerned about the health and welfare of his men, Parry successfully combatted boredom during the long Arctic winter with musical concerts (he was an accomplished fiddler), plays and skits, exercise, classes that taught his sailors to read and write, and scientific observation. He also held regular religious services. His descendant and biographer Ann Parry describes him as a "fervent, cheerful, evangelical Christian." After Parry's death in 1855, Sir Clements Markham praised him as "the beau ideal of an Arctic officer."

ABOVE Portrait of Sir William Edward Parry, 1820, painted by Samuel Drummond. National Portrait Gallery, London

Hecla and **Griper** enter
**Arctic seas on Parry's first
voyage, 1819.** From Parry,
Journal of a Voyage

Lancaster Sound. There, "in the event of its proving a strait opening to the westward, you are to use all possible means . . . to pass through it . . . and if it should be found to connect itself with the northern sea, you are to make the best of your way to Behring's Strait."

Sailing north through heavy ice, Parry pushed into Lancaster Sound, passing the imaginary line of Croker's Mountains. The expedition entered Barrow Strait, with Parry naming a large opening nearby Croker Inlet, probably in jest.

Parry was now in waters never before traversed by Europeans. "We now began to flatter ourselves," he wrote, "that we had fairly entered the Polar Sea." They had. *Hecla* and *Griper* continued westward, and on September 4, passed 110° west. Parliament had promised a £5,000 reward to the first ship to reach that position, so Parry named the nearest promontory Cape Bounty in honour of the occasion. They were now halfway through the Northwest Passage, and although they did not know it, nearly out of the Arctic archipelago.

Ice stopped their progress on September 17, at 112°51' west longitude. Parry retreated east to Melville Island, where *Hecla* and *Griper* anchored in a cove he named Winter Harbour. Their year-long sojourn was the first winter spent on the Arctic Ocean by British ships. It was, Parry wrote, not only a first for "any officer in his Majesty's navy" but also a "rare occurrence in the whole history of navigation."

Hecla and *Griper*'s topmasts were taken down, the decks were housed over with a tent made of lumber and canvas, and the ships were surrounded by blocks of ice to help insulate the hulls. During the winter, Parry kept morale high and his crew healthy, growing plants and organizing active

Entering the Northwest Passage, sailing through Barrow Strait, 1819. From Parry, *Journal of a Voyage*

Winter Harbour

One of the great landmarks of the Arctic, Edward Parry's monument at Winter Harbour has marked the anchorage of *Hecla* and *Griper* since 1820. The massive sandstone boulder stands 10 feet high, 22 feet long, and about 8 feet broad. Carved in its face is the legend: "His Britannic Majesty's Ships Hecla & Griper Commanded by W. E. Parry & M. Liddon Wintered in the adjacent harbour 1819–20." The monument marks the westernmost point reached by Parry—a position British ships would not again reach until HMS *Resolute* and *Intrepid* of Edward Belcher's expedition anchored there in 1852.

ABOVE **Parry's monument at Winter Harbour.** Parks Canada/Caroline Phillips

FACING PAGE **Close up of the inscription on Parry's monument at Winter Harbour.** Parks Canada/Caroline Phillips

Hecla and *Griper*, housed over for the winter, at **Winter Harbour, 1819.** From Parry, *Journal of a Voyage*

FACING PAGE, TOP The
crews of *Hecla* and *Griper* cut
a passage through the ice to
tow the ships into **Winter
Harbour, 1819.** From Parry,
Journal of a Voyage

FACING PAGE, BOTTOM **The
muskox, as depicted by
Lieutenant Frederick William
Beechey, an accomplished
artist and naval officer sailing
with Parry.** From Parry, *Journal
of a Voyage*

theatrical productions in which even he took
part. In addition, "to promote good humour . . .
as well as furnish amusing occupation, during the
hours of constant darkness, we set on foot a
weekly newspaper" named the *North Georgia
Gazette and Winter Chronicle*.

Total darkness lasted between November 11,
1819, and February 3, 1820. When the weather
warmed, Parry decided to make an overland trek
to explore the surrounding area. Crossing Melville
Island, he and his party reached a place where
they felt the sea resumed. In order to make sure,
they dug down—in all, 14 feet and 4 inches. "The
water" then "flowed up within fifteen inches of
the ice." It tasted enough like salt to convince
Parry he was indeed standing atop the frozen sea.

Hecla and *Griper* broke out of the ice and sailed
for home on August 1. They received a warm
reception, and Edward Parry, a hero's welcome.
He had concluded one of the most successful
voyages in the history of the quest for the
Northwest passage. The expedition ended without loss of life, opened the first leg of the passage
and pushed 600 miles west. Decades would pass
before a ship sailing from the east reached as far.

By Land to the Polar Sea, 1819–22

While Edward Parry's voyage was without undue
hardship, another, sent out under the command
of Lieutenant John Franklin, assumed Gothic
proportions. The Admiralty sent Franklin by
land to retrace Hearne's footsteps, with orders

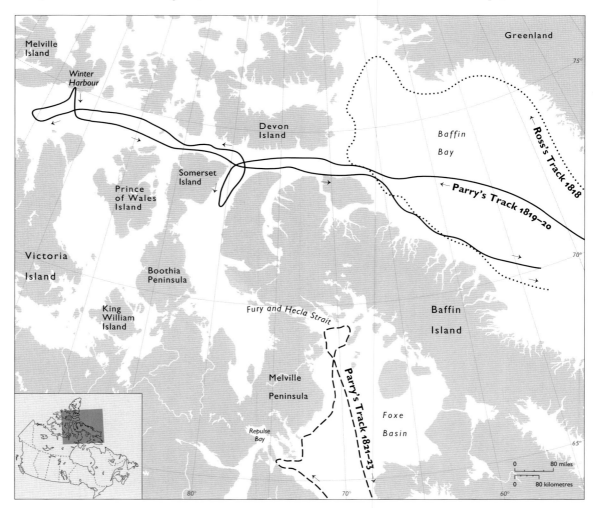

ABOVE John Franklin, a veteran of the Admiralty's first probe of the Arctic in 1818, returned to lead an ill-fated land expedition in 1819.
Vancouver Maritime Museum

FACING PAGE A scene typical of the conditions that faced Franklin and his party as they canoed along Arctic rivers. Nunavut Tourism

"to amend the very defective geography of the northern part of America" by following the Coppermine River to its mouth and then charting the coast of the Arctic Ocean.

Franklin was joined by three brother officers of the Royal Navy—surgeon John Richardson, midshipmen George Back and Robert Hood—and by seaman John Hepburn. They sailed from England on May 28, 1819, on the Hudson's Bay Company supply ship *Prince of Wales*. The ship entered the bay and anchored off York Factory, the Company's principal post in the region, on August 30.

The expedition left York Factory on September 9, working their way by water and overland to the various forts and outposts of both the Hudson's Bay Company and its rival, the North West Company. With winter setting in, they stopped at Cumberland House, an HBC post 690 miles distant from York Factory, but Franklin did not tarry long. On January 18, 1820, he headed for Fort Chipewyan.

Tracing their way north through a maze of rivers and lakes, Franklin and his men were joined by French-Canadian voyageurs and Indian guides. After descending the Yellowknife River out of Great Slave Lake, they decided to stop in late August and build a winter camp, which they named Fort Enterprise. They were now 553 miles out of Fort Chipewyan. The expedition was dealt a blow when they discovered that some supplies had been left behind, leaving them short of food and necessities. It was a disturbing harbinger.

In June 1821, Franklin and his men, joined by voyageurs and Indian guides, headed down the Coppermine River, carrying and dragging 180-pound packs and portaging their two large birchbark canoes when they could not navigate the rapids, or when ice and snags blocked their way. They reached the mouth of the river and the Arctic Ocean on the evening of July 17. With nineteen men and two canoes, Franklin set out to chart the coast. He was pleased, as were the other officers and Hepburn, to be on the sea again; it was, he noted "an element more congenial with

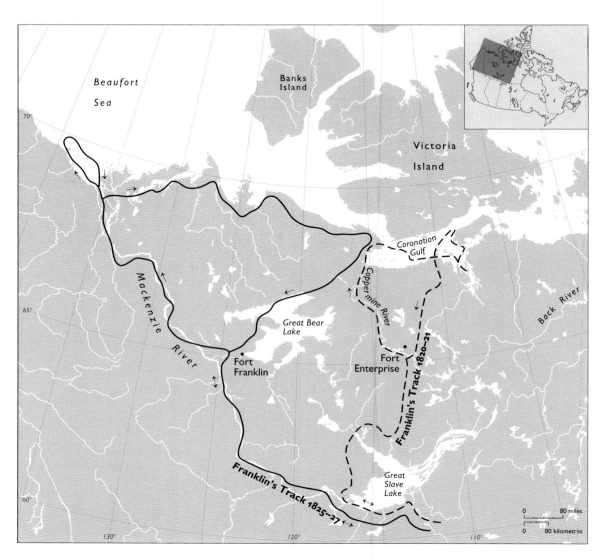

Beaufort
Sea

Banks
Island

Victoria
Island

70°

65°

60°

Mackenzie River

Copper mine River

Coronation Gulf

Back River

Great Bear Lake

Fort
Franklin

Fort
Enterprise

Franklin's Track 1820–21

Franklin's Track 1825–27

Great Slave Lake

130°   120°   110°

0   80 miles
0   80 kilometres

our habits than the fresh-water navigations, with their numerous difficulties."

They pushed east along the Arctic coast, which Franklin described as "sterile and inhospitable. . . . One trap-cliff succeeds another with tiresome uniformity." Ice was a problem, too. On July 25, the fog cleared in time to show heavy pack ice advancing on the canoes. "The coast near us was so steep and rugged that no landing . . . could be effected, and we were preserved only by some men jumping on the rocks and thrusting the ice off with poles."

In all, Franklin mapped 550 miles of coast before deciding to turn back at the end of

August; food was running low and the voyageurs were complaining loudly. He named their far-thest east position Point Turnagain and retreated with apologies in his journal to any who might consider their coastal survey too brief. On the bright side, he noted: "Our researches as far as they have gone, favour the opinion of those who contend for a North-West Passage. The general line of the coast probably runs east and west . . . and I think there is little doubt of a continued sea."

As the expedition retraced its route, Franklin continued to assess the area around Arctic and Melville Sounds and Bathurst Inlet. Naming the entire region Coronation Gulf, he ascended

Franklin's Point Turnagain.
Vancouver Maritime Museum

another river, which he named for Hood. The arduous trek was marked by what Franklin suspected was sabotage by his voyageurs. One canoe was clumsily dropped and smashed, and the other had to be discarded. Out of food and reduced to scraping lichen off the rocks and boiling it, they were in dire straits. Finding the bones and scraps of hide from a long-dead deer, the men boiled them into a soup. On other occasions, they ate their old shoes.

In a desperate race to reach Fort Enterprise, where supplies were supposed to have been cached, Franklin split his expedition into three groups on October 3. Hood, stricken with dysentery and unable to walk, was left behind with Hepburn and surgeon Richardson, who would stay to nurse him back to health. They were joined by some of the voyageurs. Back pushed ahead, as quickly as he could, to seek help from the Indians who lived near Fort Enterprise. Franklin, with the bulk of the expedition, followed.

When Franklin reached Fort Enterprise on October 11, though, he discovered it "a perfectly desolate habitation," with no Indians camped nearby and no food. A note left by Back explained that he had arrived two days earlier to find the fort empty and was in pursuit of the Indians, who were moving south. If necessary,

Fort Enterprise

Archaeologists have studied the remains of John Franklin's Fort Enterprise, scene of the tragic events of his first Arctic expedition. Located on the shores of Winter Lake and the Snare River, Fort Enterprise is some 145 miles north-northeast of Yellowknife in the Northwest Territories.

The fort's three log buildings—the officers' quarters, a cabin for the voyageurs and a store-house—formed three sides of a quadrangle. Built of logs with rough-hewn plank floors, the officers' quarters were in a 50-by-24-foot building, the roof and walls plastered with clay and the windows covered with parchment. It was divided into a main hall, three bedrooms and a kitchen. This was the setting for the final drama as the starving survivors scavenged for burnt bones and scraps of leather for food while burning the floor boards for warmth.

After the fort was abandoned on November 16, 1821, with the bodies of two of the voyageurs either buried there or left inside the storehouse, few people made their way to the site. An early visitor, one David Wheeler, stopped there in 1912 and reported that the buildings still stood. O. R. Wray of the Canadian Geological Survey visited the site in July 1932 and photographed tumbled-down fireplaces, fallen logs and the outlines of the buildings. In 1938, John Carroll, an engineer with Canada's Department of Mines and Resources, found the fort's ruins in a stand of trees.

Souvenir hunters followed, with known forays in 1948 and again in 1965 that saw them digging up the ruins. Shards of crockery, a Royal Navy button and human bones, probably the remains of one of the voyageurs, were found. Parts of the site were destroyed while unearthing these pieces of the past. Considerable damage had already been done by the time archaeologist William C. Noble visited Fort Enterprise in July 1967.

Archaeologist Timothy C. Losey excavated portions of the fort in August 1970. While "surprisingly little evidence" was visible on the surface of the ground, his excavation exposed the remains of the foundations and floor of the main building. The plank flooring had been torn up in all the rooms except the main hall, or dining area, and one bedroom, indicating that these were the rooms the men had occupied in their struggle for survival.

A number of broken and scattered artifacts were unearthed: nails, gunflints, lead shot, broken parts of guns, beads, shards of crockery, pipe bowl fragments, a metal button, iron and copper scraps, and three rolls of birchbark (possibly to repair canoes). But the bones are the most telling evidence of the tragedy. A piece of the skull of one man was discovered. Many caribou bones were also found—smashed, burnt and broken, with the marrow reamed out of the fragments. These were the remnants of the pitiable meals that had enabled the starving explorers to cling to life.

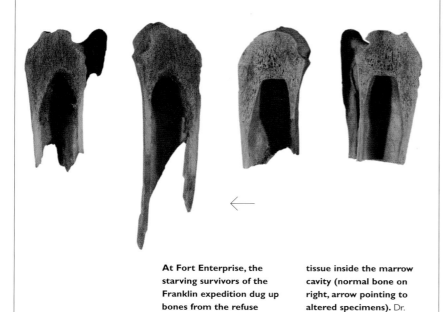

At Fort Enterprise, the starving survivors of the Franklin expedition dug up bones from the refuse trench to ream out the fatty tissue inside the marrow cavity (normal bone on right, arrow pointing to altered specimens). Dr. Timothy C. Losey, 1970

**The members of the
Franklin expedition landing
their canoe in a storm,
August 23, 1821.** From Franklin,
*Narrative of a Journey to the Shores
of the Polar Sea*

he would go as far as the North West Company outpost at Fort Providence, 150 miles south, to find food and help. All Franklin could do now was hunker down. Boiling discarded hides and burnt bones for a thin, scarcely life-sustaining soup, Franklin and his men clung precariously to life.

Richardson and Hepburn arrived at Fort Enterprise at the end of October with terrible news. One voyageur, Michel, had slowly gone insane. Two of his mates had gone missing, and, not long thereafter, Michel appeared with meat he said came from a dead wolf he had found. Hood, Richardson and Hepburn believed it had been cannibalized from the dead voyageurs. A dramatic climax was not far off. While Richardson was away seeking food and firewood, and Hepburn was not in the tent, Michel shot Hood in the back of the head. In desperation, and in fear of

their own lives, but no longer encumbered by Hood, Richardson and Hepburn marched toward Fort Enterprise with Michel. But at the first opportunity, Richardson surprised the heavily armed voyageur and shot him.

Reunited now at Fort Enterprise, the survivors grimly held on to life for the next month. Richardson later wrote of the "filth and wretchedness . . . the ghastly countenances, dilated eye-balls, and sepulchral voices" that were nearly too much to bear. The ordeal was too much for some. Three of the voyageurs died. Rescue came at last in November. Back had caught up with the Indians, and a group returned to Fort Enterprise with food. The expedition remained at the fort for the rest of the winter, rebuilding their strength, before starting east. They arrived at York Factory on July 14, 1822.

"Canoe of the Savage Islands, Hudson's Strait": a view of an Inuit hunter in his kayak, with an umiak in the background. From Parry, *Journal of a Second Voyage*

Thus ended "our long, fatiguing and disastrous travels," Franklin wrote. They had encompassed, on land and water, some 5,500 miles, and an even longer journey into the darkest depths of despair ever found in the human heart.

Edward Parry's Second Voyage, 1821–23

While John Franklin was still struggling through the wilderness, the Admiralty ordered Edward Parry back north to search in another direction for the passage. This time, Parry was to take a more southerly approach, through Prince Regent's Inlet, to avoid the heavy ice that had blocked him in 1820. The crowded *Griper* was replaced with HMS *Fury*, under Parry's com-

mand, while Lieutenant George F. Lyon was given her sister ship *Hecla*. They left on May 8, 1821, and were in the ice by July 2, sailing up past Resolution Island into Hudson Strait, heading toward the top of the bay. There, Somerset Island stood in the way of northern advance. To the west of the island lay Roes Welcome, the route by which Christopher Middleton had headed north in 1742 before turning back at Repulse Bay. To the east of the island lay Middleton's "Frozen Strait," half-forgotten, not shown on most charts and still the subject of controversy as to whether or not it existed.

Parry boldly opted for Frozen Strait. *Hecla* and *Fury* sailed past Baffin Island, through a thick fog,

Putting *Fury* and *Hecla* into winter quarters, 1821. From Parry, *Journal of a Second Voyage*

Inuit on a sled ride, as depicted by Parry's expedition artists. From Parry, *Journal of a Second Voyage*

in late August. After a day of feeling their way with constant soundings, the fog lifted to show that they had passed through the strait and were in Repulse Bay. Parry explored its shores, then headed for a large bay on Winter Island, where the ships froze in. They were just south of the Arctic Circle.

Once again, Parry settled into a winter routine of scientific observation, experimentation and theatrical amusement. A last-minute gift, "a large and handsome *phantasmagoria*, or magic lantern" also helped to amuse and delight with its illuminated scenes. "Nobody," Parry later com-

mented, "ever felt any symptoms of *ennui*."

On February 1, 1822, the men aboard *Hecla* and *Fury* reported that "a number of strange people were seen to the westward, coming towards the ships over the ice." Through his telescope, Parry saw a party of twenty-five Inuit approaching. He set out to meet them with Lyon, two other officers and two seamen. The Inuit invited the Englishmen back to their camp. Entering the igloos, Parry was astounded by their size and beauty. He was also impressed by his hosts' intelligence, charm, honesty and grace.

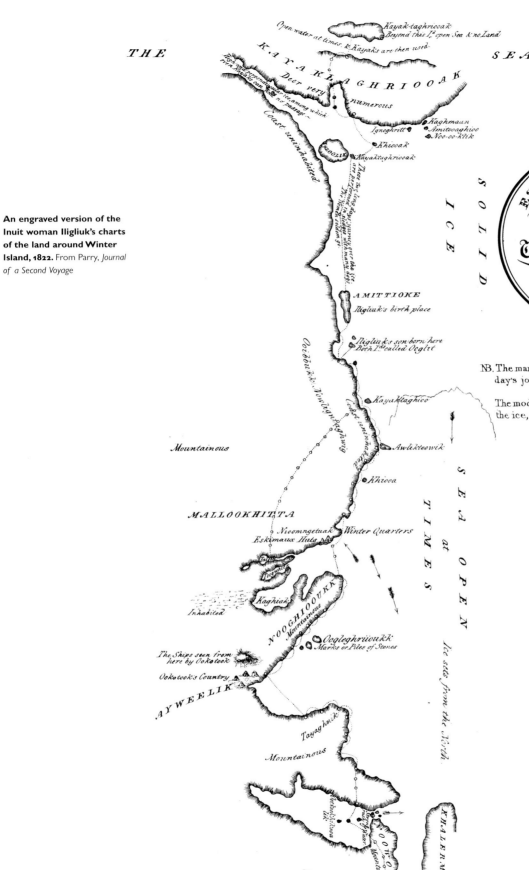

An engraved version of the Inuit woman Iligliuk's charts of the land around Winter Island, 1822. From Parry, *Journal of a Second Voyage*

THE SEA

Kayak-taghrieoak
Open water at times, & Kayak's are then used
Beyond this I.ᵈ open Sea & no Land

K A Y A K L A G H R I O O A K

Deer very numerous

High rocky precipice & the ice among which are broken can no passage

Coast uninhabited

Igneghritt
Kaghmaan
Amitwoaghioo
Noo-oo-klik

Khiooak
Kayaktaghrieoak

There two long Lakes & journey over the ice are performed in sledges with a mast, sail &c. The Water widens &c.

SOLID ICE

ESKIMAUX CHART.
№1
Drawn by
ILIGLIUK
at
Winter Island,
1822.
The Original in the possession of
Capᵗⁿ Lyon.

AMITTIOKE
Iligliuk's birth place

Iligliuk's son born here
Both I.ᵈˢ called Ooglit

Ooibooikk Nowlignitaghwig

Kayaktaghioo

NB. The marks ○ are sleeping places, or one day's journey each, and the dotted line is the track on the ice.
The mode of travelling is by sledges on the ice, and resting for the night on shore.

Mountainous

Coast uninhabited

Awlikteewik

Khiooa

S E A   a t   T I M E S   O P E N

MALLOOKHIETA

Nieomngetuak
Winter Quarters
Eskimaux Huts

Kaghiah
Inhabited

NOOGHIOOUKK
Mountainous

Oogleghriioukk
Marks or Piles of Stones

The Ships seen from here by Ookotook

Ookotook's Country

AYWEELIK

Ice sets from the North

Tayaghnek

Mountainous

KHALERMIOO

OOTOOK
Mountainous

Nannoos Country

Over the next three months, the Englishmen and the Inuit developed a close relationship. Parry befriended a boy, Toolooak, who, "one day for a couple of hours" sat in Parry's cabin, "drawing faces and animals, an occupation to which he took a great fancy." This was the first time the Inuit people of the region had ever used pencil and paper. Toolooak's drawings, as well as others by his relatives and friends, survive at the Scott Polar Research Institute to this day.

Parry was also greatly impressed by Toolooak's mother, Iligliuk. A natural musician and singer, she delighted the Englishmen with her songs, but also enjoyed listening to Parry and his men play their violins and flutes. Iligliuk also took pencil to paper to draw a map of the region for Parry. Her map showed that the ships were anchored on the eastern shores of a peninsula that was in itself a narrow isthmus, 50 miles wide, separating Hudson Bay from the Arctic Ocean. Beyond it, she reported, was "one wide-extended sea."

Parry confirmed Iligliuk's map by continuing north to the top of the Melville Peninsula. There, he reached a new body of water that he named Fury and Hecla Strait. From his vantage point, he saw much of what Iligliuk had drawn. The Royal Navy had its first confirmation, overruling condescension and prejudice, of the veracity of Inuit information. As Barrow pointed out later, "to her alone . . . is the merit due of the discovery of the extreme northern boundary of America."

Although cheered by the discovery of the strait and the view of the ocean beyond, ice prevented Parry from entering it. Frozen even in the summer, the strait was impassable. After probing the entrance, a frustrated Parry retreated, as the

Fury and Hecla Strait. From Parry, *Journal of a Second Voyage*

season was late, to winter quarters. The winter was marked by return visits by the Inuit, including Toolooak. Parry and Lyon purchased dogsleds and clothing from their Inuit friends and made a short excursion. It was a first in the annals of Arctic exploration, this remarkable experiment in "going native."

By August 1823, the ice still had not released the ships, so Parry set the men to sawing a channel. Once the ships were free of the ice, Parry sought the counsel of his officers. Three men had died the year before, and despite their best efforts, scurvy was setting in again. The officers were of one mind; the men might not last a third winter. And so the expedition turned for home. "I no longer considered it prudent or justifiable, upon the slender chance of eventual success" in forcing through the icy strait, Parry wrote.

As John Barrow and the Admiralty assessed the records of the various expeditions, it seemed obvious, from the tantalizing glimpses thus far afforded, that a Northwest Passage could be found. All that was needed was enough men and ships to enter the Arctic from a number of directions.

A Push in All Directions

CHAPTER 5

The poor ship cracked and trembled violently; and no one could say the next minute would not be her last, and indeed his own, too, for with her our means of safety would probably perish. —GEORGE BACK, 1838

THE HOPES of the Admiralty for a final resolution to the quest for the Northwest Passage rested on its four-pronged assault on the Arctic in 1824–27. Four expeditions were assembled from the burgeoning ranks of the Royal Navy's Arctic veterans. John Franklin would again trek overland and follow the Mackenzie River to the sea. Frederick William Beechey, a veteran of Parry's voyages, would sail to the Pacific, then through the Bering Strait, and push east to rendezvous with Franklin. George Lyon would head for Repulse Bay and Winter Island, then strike west, overland, to Franklin's Point Turnagain. Edward Parry would go out to Lancaster Sound, then sail south along Prince Regent Inlet. It was hoped that the inlet would link up with the open seas he had earlier sighted from the western end of Fury and Hecla Strait, then pass south of the Boothia Peninsula to connect to the channel that Franklin had canoed.

John Franklin and Frederick Beechey, 1824–27

Franklin, who had returned home to England to regain his health, had just published an account of his first expedition. Hitherto, the narratives of the various voyages and expeditions had been restrained and scientific, extending the frontiers of knowledge. Franklin's book, in the words of historian Maurice Hodgson, presented 'a new Arctic: starvation, murder and cannibalism, the extremities of human suffering."

To avoid a repetition of the previous disaster—only nine of Franklin's twenty-man party had survived the ordeal—the Admiralty provided more supplies and equipment than were needed. The preparations took a year, and the routes were planned carefully, with caches of food laid out for the expedition. The rations were described by Franklin: "a quantity of wheaten-flour, arrowroot, macaroni, portable-soup, chocolate, essence of coffee, sugar and tea, calculated to last two years, was . . . made up into packages of eighty-five pounds and covered with three layers of prepared waterproof canvas."

The Admiralty also provided four specially built boats: three mahogany and ash double-enders, and a light, ash-framed, canvas boat named *Walnut-Shell*. Franklin brought a larger party of officers (including John Richardson, George Back, E. N. Kendall and Thomas Drummond), four Royal Marines and a group of sailors, so as not to rely on voyageurs alone. An advance party departed to make preparations and

FACING PAGE *Fury* **ashore and wrecked at Fury Beach on Edward Parry's third voyage in 1825.** From Parry, *Journal of a Third Voyage*

RIGHT **Sextant, nineteenth century.** Vancouver Maritime Museum

ready the winter quarters several months before
Franklin and the bulk of the expedition left
Britain. Franklin was taking no chances.

After sailing to New York to begin his journey north, Franklin wrote home to his ailing wife
in April 1825: "With what heartfelt pleasure shall
I embrace you . . . on my return!" He told her
that a silk Union Jack she had made was "yet snug
in the box." He then noted that Back had come
in—and the letter stops. At the bottom of the
page, in anguish, he scrawled: "The distressing
intelligence of my dear wife's death has just
reached me." Eleanor Porden had married
Franklin after his return from his first overland
expedition. She had borne him a daughter, but
taken ill. Suspecting death was near, she con-
cealed it from Franklin and encouraged him to
leave. She died six days after he sailed.

Although shaken by news of Eleanor's death,
Franklin set out. His party reached Fort
Chipewyan in mid-July, began the descent of the
Mackenzie River in August and by mid-month
reached the mouth. Standing on the highest
promontory, Franklin looked out on the sea "in
all its majesty, entirely free from ice and without
any visible obstruction to navigation." As his men
pitched camp, Franklin raised the silk flag
Eleanor had given him: "I will not attempt to
describe my emotions as it expanded to the
breeze."

The party retreated to the winter quarters
prepared by the advance party. Fort Franklin, as
it was called, over Franklin's objection (he
wanted to call it Fort Reliance) was home to
fifty-one people through the winter. In the summer of 1826, the expedition split into two parties. One, under Franklin, would push west and
follow the coast until they rendezvoused with
Beechey's expedition. The other, under
Richardson, would push east to the mouth of the
Coppermine River.

Franklin reached the coast and commenced his
voyage, encountering a large group of Inuit on
the way. In their eagerness to acquire the goods

that the expeditiion had brought for trade, the
Inuit rushed the boats and desperately took what
they could, even going so far as to cut buttons off
coats of the men wearing them and persisting in
seizing valuable items even as the marines and
sailors beat them back with the butts of their

"Fall of an Iceberg." From *The Arctic World*

muskets. Cool heads prevailed on both sides, and after a struggle that lasted several hours, Franklin withdrew. He named the place Pillage Point.

Rowing, sailing and at times wading through the icy waters, Franklin's men worked their way up the coast toward Alaska. Weather and ice forced Franklin to turn back on August 16, at a spot he named Return Reef. He was only 160 miles—but hard, ice-blocked miles—from Point Barrow, where Beechey was waiting.

Meanwhile, sailing through Bering Strait in HMS *Blossom*, Frederick Beechey followed his

Griper, commanded by
Captain George F. Lyon on
his 1824 Arctic voyage, in
Hudson Strait. From Lyon, A
Brief Narrative

instructions to push past Cook's Icy Cape in
order, hopefully, to meet up with Franklin. A
barge from *Blossom* surveyed the shoreline, traded
with the Eskimos along the Alaska coast, and left
messages and caches for Franklin before reaching
the northern point they named for Sir John
Barrow. When Beechey left on August 26, he was
not aware of how close he and Franklin had come
to meeting. But Franklin was wise to retreat.
Storms and heavy surf nearly wrecked him on
the return journey.

When Franklin and Richardson reunited at
Fort Franklin in September, they compared notes
and charts. In all they had mapped some 1,500
miles of coastline. After wintering in for the end
of 1826 and into 1827, the expedition returned
home in September. Franklin basked in the
knowledge that his maps had considerably
expanded Britain's understanding of the passage.

Beechey had also met with some success, but
the expeditions led by Lyon and Parry were not
so fortunate.

George Lyon's Failed Attempt, 1824

The Admiralty ordered George F. Lyon, commander of *Hecla* on Edward Parry's second voyage, to take the brig *Griper* and winter on the
coast of the Melville Peninsula. In the spring, he
was to journey overland to the shores of the
polar sea. From there, Lyon was to "proceed
westerly, by land, or by water, as circumstances
may admit, until you shall arrive at Point Turnagain," then return to his ship. His survey would
fill in more of the map.

Sailing in June 1824, Lyon made his way
across the Atlantic in company with the surveying vessel *Snap*, which carried the expedition's
extra supplies. *Griper* was a poor sailer, and every
so often *Snap* had to take the brig under tow. The
two vessels arrived off the entrance to Hudson
Strait in early August. *Snap* offloaded the extra
supplies into the overcrowded *Griper*, which sank
lower and lower in the water.

Griper carried on alone through the icy
waters. The situation worried Lyon: "I felt most

forcibly the want of an accompanying ship, if not to help us, at least to break the death-like stillness of the scene." While Parry had pushed into Repulse Bay by taking the "Frozen Strait" to the east of Southampton Island, Lyon tried Roes Welcome to the west. Then, on September 1, *Griper* sailed through heavy fog and rough seas into shallow water. Unable to control the ship, Lyon anchored. The tide was falling, and the wind lashed the shallow water into waves that swept the decks. Lyon ordered the crew to ready the boats and prepare to abandon ship.

As they watched the seas, Lyon and his men realized that only the largest boat stood any chance of surviving. It was, commented Lyon, "too evident that no human powers could save us." Finally, with the tide all the way out, *Griper* lay to with only six feet of water under her keel. The waves, now breakers rushing to the exposed beach, alternately lifted the ship and dropped her onto the bottom with crashing blows that "struck with great violence." The men stood huddled in

small groups and prayed. Some tried to catch a brief nap, as no one had slept for over twenty-four hours. But all seemed lost.

Somehow *Griper* held together, and when the tide turned and rose, Lyon was able to claw the brig out of the anchorage, which he piously named the Bay of God's Mercy. But the stormy weather was far from over. On the evening of September 12, sleet froze into the rigging and flying snow coated the deck with a foot of ice. The sea washed freely over the frozen deck, soaking the men. "The temporary warmth it gave while it washed over us was most painfully checked by its almost immediately freezing on our clothes." As the seas heaved the tiny brig, Lyon confessed "I never beheld a darker night."

The next day, the anchor cables parted, leaving the brig adrift. The crew sprang to stations, hauling on the frozen ropes. Lyon ordered them to turn about. While beating their way south, he decided the only possible course was to run for home. His men were beaten, the ship damaged and the conditions too trying. *Griper* reached Britain on November 10, much to the surprise of the Admiralty.

Barrow publicly defended Lyon: "The voyage along this eastern coast of North America has been tried many times, and always found more or less disastrous." The hallmark of Lyon's attempt, Barrow wrote, was that the men of *Griper* displayed "a fine example of manly resolution under the most distressing difficulties." However, Lyon was silently condemned and never again commanded a ship. His former commander, Parry, in a personal letter, confided that it was a "too common attempt on the part of the Admiralty, to let the blame for failure lie on any shoulders but their own. This is certainly the case now, with respect to the *Griper*, a vessel of such lubberly, shameful construction."

Edward Parry's Third Voyage, 1824–25

The fourth prong was led by Edward Parry, who, upon his return to Britain in October 1823, had told his superiors that he was ready to try for the Northwest Passage again. "I considered it well worth another trial . . . we had narrowed the ground of enquiry, by having proved, at least where the thing was not to be done." They agreed, and Parry recommissioned *Hecla* while Henry Hoppner, who had sailed with Parry since Ross's voyage, commissioned *Fury*. The ships sailed on May 19, 1824. Parry's instructions were to push up Davis Strait and enter Lancaster Sound, then Barrow's Strait. At the top of Baffin Island, they were to turn southwest, enter Prince Regent Inlet and continue on until they linked up with Lyon, Franklin or Beechey.

Entering Davis Strait in late June, *Hecla* and *Fury* encountered many huge icebergs, an unmistakable sign of a bad ice year. Parry noted: "We counted from the deck, at one time, no less than one hundred and three of these immense bodies, some of them from 100 to 200 feet in height, above the sea, and it was necessary, in one or two instances, to tow the ships clear of them with the

boats." The ice thickened, and by mid-July, progress was hard won, with the crew constantly "heaving, warping, or sawing" through the ice. By the end of the month, they had covered only 70 miles. On August 1, *Hecla* was almost lost when the ice pushed up on both sides and under the bottom, rolling the ship onto her beam ends, with the masts almost touching the ice. It would have "crushed a vessel of ordinary strength," wrote Parry. But *Hecla* survived the "nipping" of the ice, and the expedition continued to struggle westward for another eight weeks.

Entering Lancaster Sound in September, Parry had almost reached his goal of Prince Regent Inlet when fresh ice, forming on the sea, caught the ships and began pushing them inexorably east. A gale broke up the ice, allowing Parry to find a toehold on the eastern shores of the inlet, near the entrance. They wintered at a small harbour named Port Bowen, which Parry had surveyed in 1819. Scientific observation, music, "masquerades," and a school for the seamen again formed their winter routine. Land parties also explored the surrounding country. "All is dreary monotonous whiteness," Parry wrote. "Not merely for days or weeks, but for more than half a year together. Which-ever way the eye is turned, it meets . . . inanimate stillness. . . . In the very silence there is a deadness with which a human spectator *appears out of keeping*. The presence of man seems an intrusion on the dreary solitude of this wintry desert."

Release from the ice usually came in the brief summer, when the sun melted the pack in the shallows. The shade from the high cliffs around Port Bowen, however, kept the ice from thawing completely, and in early July 1825, Parry had the men saw channels through the ice and tow the ships into open water. Working their way down the inlet, along the shores of Somerset Island, "We found ourselves upon ground not hitherto explored," said Parry. "The labours of a bad summer, and the tedium of a long winter, were forgotten."

But by month's end, the ice had moved in close to shore and trapped the ships against high cliffs, "which here rise to a perpendicular height of between four and five hundred feet." The men shifted the ships as best they could to face the ice and anchored them as far offshore as possible, but a gale blew in and drove the ice and ships toward shore. Some of *Hecla*'s hawsers snapped and a bulwark was torn away. *Fury* was pushed onto the beach, but the crews of the two ships were able to pull her free.

The next day brought more wind and more ice, and *Fury* grounded again. The ice forced its way around her hull, which opened to the sea. After drifting and pumping constantly for forty-eight hours, the exhausted crew of *Fury* were relieved when Parry and Hoppner selected a small, narrow beach for a desperate effort at saving her. It was a "wild and insecure" spot to attempt to beach *Fury* and try to repair her, Parry later said, but it was their only chance.

The heavily laden *Fury* was unloaded on the beach by both crews working around the clock. Heaps of supplies, casks and crates littered the narrow beach. Lightened and pumped, the ship was inspected. The news was not good; the sternpost and forefoot, at each end of the ship, were twisted and broken, and the keel was torn up. The damage was severe. It was clear that *Fury* might not make it home.

At the same time, the large icebergs that were sheltering the two ships from the pack ice were melting and grinding away, leaving them exposed. *Hecla*, her hull already strained by encounters with the ice, and now quite possibly the only way home, was in danger. While Parry and Hoppner still hoped to save *Fury*, their duty now lay in getting *Hecla* ready to run away.

This was done, and the crews then returned to the stranded *Fury* and began to reload the ship. After loading some 50 tons, the men were called to dinner. While they were eating, the dreaded onslaught of ice began. Parry called all hands to stations, and *Hecla* moved away from *Fury*.

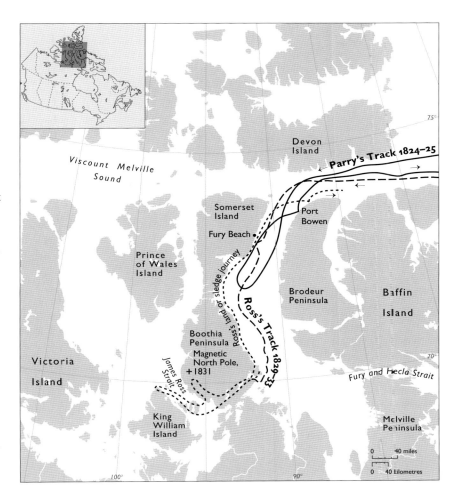

The ice pushed the stranded *Fury* onto the beach, twisting her hull. As *Hecla*, with both crews aboard, moved away, the stranded hulk receded into the distance.

After moving farther south, to a headland Parry named Cape Garry, *Hecla* encountered open seas. "Had we now been at liberty to take advantage of the favourable prospect before us, I have little doubt we should without much difficulty have made considerable progress," Parry wrote. He did not realize that the inlet ended in a dead end, with only a narrow, ice-clogged strait connecting it to the west. But any thoughts of pressing on were now forgotten. After being held off by the ice, *Hecla* returned to the spot now named Fury Beach. The wrecked *Fury* lay on her side, her holds full of water. The officers nonetheless carefully surveyed the wreck with the ship's carpenters and rowed back in silence to report that the situation was "hopeless." The crowded *Hecla* retreated, reaching Britain in November.

Fury Beach today. Parks
Canada/ Caroline Phillips

Fury's Cache

When HMS *Hecla* sailed from Fury Beach on August 25, 1825, the hulk of HMS *Fury*, lying on her side close to the water's edge, was left behind. The next time Europeans visited the site, *Fury* was gone, carried away by the ice and the sea. But the tons of provisions that had been unloaded from her remained on the beach. John Ross described how the "canisters" or tins of preserved food lay "piled up in two heaps; but though quite exposed to all the changes of the climate, for four years, they had not suffered in the slightest degree. There had been no water to rust them, and the security of their joinings had prevented the bears from smelling their contents." He wondered: "Is it possible that this may yet be, some thousand years hence, that the ever-during frost of Boothia Felix may preserve the equally ever-during canisters of the *Fury*, and thus deliver down to a remote posterity the dinners cooked in London during the reign of George the Fourth?"

Barrels and casks of other provisions also lay on the beach, all in good condition, and piles of sails "were not only dry, but seemed as if they had never been wetted." Ross later used the sails to construct Somerset House, his shelter for the winter of 1834. The boxes of tallow candles had been eaten by mice, but all else was in relatively good order except the tents that bears had mauled and pushed aside to get at the food. Portions of *Fury* were also found, including a spare mizzen-topmast and the "chain cable and the carronades."

Several parties from ships searching for Franklin between 1849 and 1857 visited Fury Beach, taking provisions and souvenirs. By the time Parks Canada archaeologists surveyed Fury Beach and the scattered remains of the *Fury*'s supplies in 1977 and 1978, not much remained. Circles of stones once used to hold down canvas tents, the outlines of Somerset House, and piles of broken wood, tins and iron hoops from the casks of supplies were the only visible evidence. Like so many other historic and archaeological sites in the Arctic, Fury Beach has suffered from the depredations of relic hunters and vandals.

Lid from a flour barrel, Fury Beach. Vancouver Maritime Museum/Michael Paris

Scottish-born John Ross is one of the more fascinating characters in the saga of the Northwest Passage.

John Ross entered the Royal Navy in 1786 at the age of nine to serve as a "first class volunteer." After his introduction to the sea, young Ross entered the service of the East India Company, returning to the navy in 1799 as a midshipman. During the Napoleonic Wars, Ross rose in rank and showed great bravery. In one skirmish, armed with only a sword, he led his men into a boat of Spanish soldiers and captured it, although he was bayoneted, cut badly on the head, and had both legs and one arm broken.

His critical error in assuming Lancaster Sound was blocked by mountains—an optical illusion that his fellow officers did not agree with—seemed likely to doom his Arctic career. But he rebounded, with private support and buoyed by his own strong character, ego and courage, to command the first steamer into the far north. Trapped in the ice with his men, Ross nearly died, but managed to lead them, including his second-in-command and nephew, James Clark Ross, to safety. In his old age, at seventy-two, he returned to the Arctic in a valiant but failed effort to find and rescue his old friend and colleague, John Franklin.

John Ross was knighted for his achievements—and for his public popularity, no doubt, after his return from "the dead" in 1834, when he and his men were rescued from the Arctic. Ross could be both engaging and infuriating. Controversy dogged him as he battled his detractors, including John Barrow. He was contentious up to the time of his death in November 1856, taking swipes at the Admiralty and his nephew James over their failure to rescue John Franklin.

Rear Admiral M. J. Ross, a descendant, notes that John Ross was eccentric, friendly, "strangely naive at times," and "though his manifest shortcomings cannot be denied, they have unfortunately tended to obscure much that was admirable in his character."

The quest for the Northwest Passage had hitherto been marked with considerable luck, some hardship and a few lives lost. But now came the loss of a ship, and although Parry commented that "the only real cause for wonder has been our long exemption from such a catastrophe," the wreck of *Fury* weighed hard. When the Admiralty assessed the results of its much anticipated four-point push, it saw only failure. The next voyage in search of the passage was a private endeavour, launched in part to regain a reputation lost on the first push west in 1818.

The Return of John Ross, 1829–33

Ten years after his active naval career ended with his failure to penetrate Lancaster Sound, John Ross appealed to the Admiralty for another Arctic command. An advocate of the then-developing steam engine, he asserted that a steamship was the ideal vessel for navigating the Northwest Passage. However, interest had waned, and in 1828 Parliament repealed the reward of £20,000 for the discovery of the passage. While signalling the government's disinterest, this action opened the door for private enterprise now that the "unseemly" prospect of competing with His Majesty's ships and officers for a government prize was cleared away. In this new atmosphere, John Ross approached an old friend, Felix Booth, the wealthy distiller of Booth's Gin, to fund an expedition. Booth agreed to pay £10,000, to which Ross added £3,000 of his own money.

In June 1828, Ross purchased a small, 85-ton paddlewheel steamer named *Victory* and refitted her for an Arctic voyage. This included experimental boilers, designed by manufacturer John Braithwaite and a young Swedish inventor, John Ericsson. Ross took along his nephew, James Clark Ross, who had sailed with Parry on all of his expeditions.

Victory, with four officers and nineteen men, many of them drawn from the ranks of the Royal Navy, sailed from Britain on June 13, 1829. Hampered by stormy weather and constant problems

James Clark Ross

Veteran of both Arctic and Antarctic voyages, scientist and naval officer, James Clark Ross was born in 1800. He was the third son of explorer John Ross's older brother, George. James entered the Royal Navy in 1812, serving under his uncle John Ross aboard the sloop *Briseis* in the Baltic. When the elder Ross assumed command of the Baffin Bay expedition in 1818, he took young James with him, launching a polar career that spanned three decades.

After sailing to the Arctic with John Ross in *Isabella*, James served on all four of Edward Parry's Arctic expeditions. In 1827, Ross and Parry reached what was then Britain's farthest northward reach, 82°45'.

The two Rosses reunited in 1829, on John Ross's voyage to the Boothia Peninsula in the steamer *Victory*. The expedition also sought to pinpoint the north magnetic pole. James, who had learned magnetic surveying in 1818 from Edward Sabine, lieutenant and scientist aboard *Isabella*, had since honed his science under Parry. Indeed, Ross's principal biographer, his great-grandson Rear Admiral M. J. Ross, credits the years

James spent with Parry as critical, formative influences on both his character and career. He found his uncle's character and actions lacking on their joint expedition of 1829–33, and relations between the two were strained thereafter.

At the end of 1835, he took command of the ship *Cove* and set out to find and rescue a group of Arctic whalers trapped in the ice. At the end of what proved to be a difficult voyage, Ross was offered a knighthood, which he declined. From 1837 to 1839, he was taken up with a magnetic survey of Great Britain.

In 1839–43, Ross, with the bombs *Erebus* and *Terror*, surveyed the edges of the Antarctic. He was not able to penetrate into the continent, but his discovery of an opening in the great ice sheet named for him showed the way for later explorers. James Ross then returned home to a knighthood, marriage, and retirement from the sea. The disappearance of Sir John Franklin, as well as F. R. M. Crozier, another friend, took James back to the Arctic in 1848–49. His voyage in HMS *Enterprise* was widely viewed as dis-

appointing by the public, but one of his greatest achievements in the search was his selection of Francis Leopold McClintock, who began his Arctic career as Ross's second lieutenant. Ross introduced McClintock to sledge travel, and the young officer, became, perhaps, the greatest sledge traveller in the Royal Navy. It was McClintock who, on a sledge trip to King William Island in 1858–59, ascertained finally what had befallen Franklin.

Ross's health was shaken by his last expedition, and he spent his declining years at home, with his family. He died on April 3, 1862, leaving a legacy of bold endeavour and scientific research undertaken in extreme circumstances at both ends of the world.

Portrait of James Clark Ross, painted by Stephen Pearce, 1850. National Portrait Gallery, London

TOP **John Ross's *Victory* at Felix Harbour.** From Ross, *Narrative of a Second Voyage*

BOTTOM **Felix Harbour today.** James M. Savelle

with the steam machinery, *Victory* reached Davis Strait in July. So as not to rely on the engines, Ross rerigged *Victory*'s masts with spars and sails from the wrecked whaler *Rookwood*, which lay abandoned at Holsteinsborg. He then headed for Lancaster Sound. On August 12, they were at the entrance to Prince Regent Inlet. Ross's intent was to push down the inlet, past where Parry had lost *Fury*, toward the open waters *Hecla* had found before turning back.

Working south through the inlet, *Victory* sailed past *Hecla*'s southernmost position and into new waters. They were now in an open body that Ross named the Gulf of Boothia; the land to the west he named Boothia Felix, both in honour of the expedition's patron. When he stopped for the winter on the shores of Boothia Felix, Ross had penetrated 150 miles farther south than Parry. There, at Felix Harbour, *Victory* was frozen in. The steam engine, which had never worked

well, was now, in Ross's opinion, "not merely useless" but "a serious encumbrance, since it occupied, with its fuel, two-thirds of our tonnage, in weight and measurement." The crew dismantled the machinery and hauled it ashore.

Ross was disappointed that he had not been able to explore farther south; for all he knew, the passage lay just beyond the horizon. But now the ice had come, "the prison door was shut upon us," and a long winter awaited them.

The expedition received a boost in early January 1830, when a party of Netsilik Inuit encountered the frozen-in *Victory*. Ross ordered his men to drop their guns and shouted "welcome" in Inuktitut. "On this, they threw their knives and spears in the air in every direction, returning the shout *Aja*, and extending their arms to show that they were also without weapons." The two groups embraced, and James Ross, with his years of experience in the Arctic, served as the interpreter.

The remains of *Victory*'s steam engine at Felix Harbour today. James M. Savelle

The Inuit Remember Ross

The Arviligjuarmiut people of Pelly Bay told anthropologist Knud Rasmussen about their first meeting with John Ross and the crew of *Victory*:

Members of Ross's expedition meet the Netsilik, January 1830. From Ross, *Narrative of a Second Voyage*

They tell that John Ross' ship was first seen early in the winter by a man named Aviluktoq, who was out sealing; when he caught sight of the great ship lying like a rock out in the middle of a small bay, his curiosity at first made him approach to see what it could be; for he had never noticed it before. But when he saw the ship's high masts he thought it was a great spirit and fled. All that evening and night the men considered what they should do, but as they were afraid that the big spirit might destroy them if they did not forestall it, they set out next day to attack it, armed with harpoons and bows. Then they discovered that human figures were walking about it, and they hid behind a block of ice to see what sort of people these could be. They had heard of kinsmen who in far distant lands had met white men, but they themselves had never done so. However, the figures around the ship had also seen them and made their way over the ice towards the ice blocks behind which they were hiding. They saw that the strangers must be the famous white men of whom they had heard so much talk and who were said to have come from the offspring of a girl in their own country and a dog. All the Arviligjuarmiut now wished to show that they were not afraid, and came out from their place of concealment. The white men at once laid their weapons on the ice, and the Eskimos followed suit. The meeting was a cordial one, with both embraces and what each party took to be assurances of friendship, for of course they could not understand a word of each other's tongue. The Eskimos went along with this great, wonderful ship and received precious gifts such as nails, sewing needles and knives, in fact everything they could not get in the country itself. And the white men seemed to have such an abundance of wood that they could even live in it—indeed, however incredible it may sound, they lived in a hollowed-out floating island of wood that was full of iron and everything else that was precious in their own country.

Netsilik winter camp, 1830, drawn by John Ross. From Ross, *Narrative of a Second Voyage*

The expedition established good relations with the Inuit, even to providing a wooden leg for a hunter, Tulluahiu, who had lost his leg to a bear attack. The Inuit, when questioned, showed the visiting Europeans the extent of their knowledge of the land. One informant, Ikmallik, was shown their chart of the inlet and gulf, and with pencil in hand added the rest of the shoreline. Ross now saw that he had sailed into a dead end; to the east lay the Melville Peninsula and Fury and Hecla Strait. Between March and June, James Ross made a series of sledge journeys with Inuit guides to examine the surrounding territory, adding detail to the expedition's maps.

Traversing the Boothia Peninsula, James Ross reached the shores of the sea on the other side. He then crossed to what he believed to be another peninsula, "King William Land" (it was later found to be an island). Ross named the northernmost promontory Cape Felix, and the next point, just as they turned back, Victory Point. From there, he looked west and saw another point, which he named Point Franklin, in honour of the earlier explorer. He was, at that moment, only 222 nautical miles from Franklin's Point Turnagain. But the time had come to return to the ship.

As Ross retreated, he had doubts that he was on the mainland. Perhaps this was a "chain of islands." The frozen sea and the low, snow-covered islands all merged together into a "dazzling mass of white," and the irregular, broken ice on the sea could be mistaken for land (Ross was actually on King William Island). As he passed its northern end and nearby Matty's Island, then turned east for the Boothia Peninsula, haze obscured the horizon. Thinking he saw the land continue, Ross terminated the strait on his chart with question marks. His uncle, eager to declare the strait closed, named the area Pocte's Bay. In fact, the strait continued, and John Ross's notation, closing off the waters around the island, was to play a significant, if not fatal, role in the future.

Two Inuit, Ikmallik and Apelagliu, drawing a chart for Ross in the cabin of Victory. From Ross, *Narrative of a Second Voyage*

The summer breakup of the ice came late, and when it did, *Victory* could not be moved far. Constantly grounding on the shallows, the steamer was anchored for a second winter after covering just four miles. The winter was long and difficult, for the Inuit did not return until April 1831. Sledging parties, led by both Rosses, continued to explore the surrounding land, but it was one of James's trips in May to June 1831 that proved significant. He crossed the Boothia Peninsula with instruments to measure magnetic variation. On previous voyages, the variation had shown that the north magnetic pole lay in this general area, and now Ross determined to fix its location.

On June 1, 1831, at 8 A.M., James Ross took a final set of readings and fixed the north magnetic pole at 70°5'17" north latitude, 96°46'45" seconds west longitude. "Nature had erected here no monument to denote the spot which she had chosen as the centre of one of her great and dark powers," Ross wrote, so "amidst mutual congratulations," he and his party "fixed the British flag on the spot and took possession of the North Magnetic Pole, and its surrounding territory, in the name of Great Britain." It was the high point of the expedition.

When the ice freed *Victory* on August 28, the steamer, with sails set, managed to work only some 10 miles northeast, after grounding and breaking the rudder. The third winter quarters, which they named Victory Harbour, marked the end of the line for the ship. Ross realized that *Victory* would have to be abandoned and that the men would have to take to the land. Supplies were running out, and scurvy was setting in, killing one man. Among the symptoms of scurvy is the reopening of old wounds. John Ross, a veteran of several battles, had been wounded

Hunting a muskox. From Ross, *Narrative of a Second Voyage*

The North Magnetic Pole

The earth's magnetic fields criss-cross the globe, fluctuating in intensity and shifting as they run from north to south, east to west. Their maximum intensity is at the equator and at each pole. But the magnetic poles are not located at 90° north and south of the geographic north and south poles, as the ebb and flow of the earth's magnetic fields move constantly across the top and bottom of the world.

One of the major scientific goals of British explorers in the Arctic was to measure magnetism and to plot the location of the north magnetic pole. Using a series of instruments, Edward Parry, John Franklin and Edward Sabine discovered that it was close to 70° north latitude and 98°30' west longitude— right in the region where they sought the Northwest Passage.

James Clark Ross, sailing to the vicinity of those coordinates with his uncle John Ross's expecition, had the opportunity to find the north magnetic pole. On June 2, 1831, James reached the location, at a low spot on the coast of the Boothia Peninsula. Even with his simple instruments, he was able measure the fact that the pole was moving even as he stood there.

The shifting of the north magnetic pole was confirmed in 1904 by Roald Amundsen. His measurements showed the pole had moved to 70°30' north, and 95°20' west, or 40 miles northeast of where Ross had found it seventy-three years earlier. The pole continues to move, and now the magnetic forces converge much farther north, off Byam Martin Island.

The remains of the cairn built in 1831 by James Clark Ross at the north magnetic pole. John Harrington

thirteen times. Now, in the fastness of the Arctic winter, his scars opened and bled. The time to escape was at hand.

Throughout the winter, the men made preparations to abandon *Victory* and sledge north, carrying the ship's boats part of the way. Their goal, stated Ross, "was to proceed to a certain distance with a stock of provisions and the boats, and there deposit them for the purpose of advancing more easily afterwards . . . the object now was to proceed to Fury Beach, not only for supplies, but to get possession of the boats there; failing which, our own would be put into a position on which we could fall back." On May 28, 1832, *Victory* was abandoned. "The colours were . . . hoisted and nailed to the mast, we drank a parting glass to our poor ship."

The "Pole"

The "North Pole" now rests in the collections of the National Maritime Museum in Greenwich, England. The pole is actually a boat's jackstaff, 6 feet. 8 inches high and on average an inch in diameter. Painted blue/green, with a gilded circular knob at its top, the jackstaff separates into two pieces, one fitting into the other's brass socket.

James Clark Ross took this jackstaff with him when he fixed the location of the north magnetic pole and stuck it into the frozen ground to mark the site. The brief biography of Ross in the *Arctic Navy List* takes great pains to highlight the fact that he "planted the Union Jack on the North Magnetic Pole." Ross bequeathed the historic jackstaff to Commander Arthur Ross, who in turn left it to his nephew, Rear Admiral M. J. Ross, who donated it to the National Maritime Museum in 1986.

This simple piece of painted wood and brass, resting in its display case, is a tangible reminder that the search for the Northwest Passage was also a quest for knowledge, and that scientific observation played an important role in Britain's Arctic expeditions.

***Victory* frozen in at Victory Harbour.** From Ross, *Narrative of a Second Voyage*

**Victory Harbour today,
hemmed by ice.** James M.
Savelle

After a hard trip north, the men reached Fury Beach on July 1. An advance party, led by James Ross, had already ascertained that *Fury*'s boats remained on the beach, so there was no need to turn back for *Victory*'s. At the beach, they built a shelter, a 31-by-16-foot wood frame and canvas building they named Somerset House. They remained for a month while the boats were re-paired, rigged and readied to sail up the inlet and into Baffin Bay, where they hoped to find whaling ships. Leaving the beach on August 1 in three boats, the men fought the ice and weather for the next two months, camping in the open as they slowly worked their way north. Forced to return to Fury Beach, the exhausted men reached Somerset House on October 7 and settled in for a fourth winter, during which a second man died. Once again, the crew were thankful for *Fury*'s stores left on the beach by Parry and Hoppner in 1824.

Leaving Somerset House on July 8, 1833, they again headed north, reaching Lancaster Sound in mid-August. Then, on August 26, they sighted a sail while resting in a small harbour just west of Navy Board Inlet. "No time . . . was lost: the boats were launched, and signals made," Ross

Piece of hardtack from Fury Beach, carried off by James Clark Ross as a souvenir.
Vancouver Maritime Museum/Michael Paris

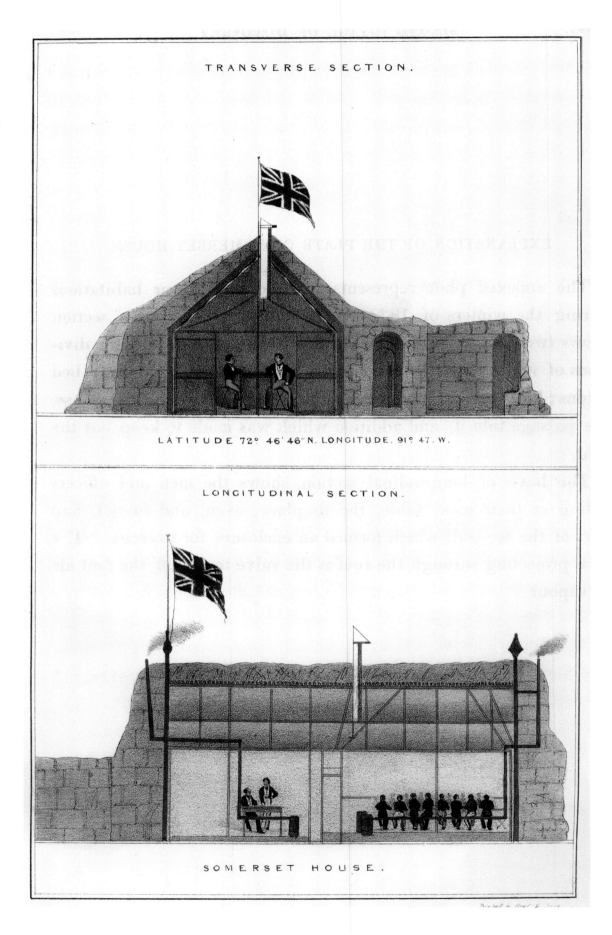

Somerset House, the refuge for Ross's stranded men at Fury Beach. From Ross, *Narrative of a Second Voyage*

LATITUDE 72° 46′ 46″ N. LONGITUDE. 91° 47. W.

LONGITUDINAL SECTION.

SOMERSET HOUSE.

recorded. After a frustrating morning of chasing the ship, it suddenly turned to and lowered a boat. "The mate in command addressed us, by presuming that we had met with some misfortune and lost our ship. This being answered in the affirmative, I requested to know the name of the vessel . . . it was 'the *Isabella* of Hull, once commanded by Captain Ross,' on which I stated I was the identical man in question." Ross noted, with relish, that "the mate, who commanded this boat . . . was . . . astonished" and "he assured me that I had been dead two years."

The expedition reached Britain on October 18. Both Rosses were showered with many honours, including a royal audience, a knighthood for John, payment of salaries by the Admiralty even though it had been a private expedition, and a promotion to captain for James. John Ross's reputation was redeemed, and James Clark Ross was honoured for his "discovery" of the north magnetic pole.

George Back's Rescue Attempt, 1833–35

When no news was received from the Ross expedition by 1832, plans for a search party were organized. George Back, veteran of three of Franklin's expeditions, was selected to lead an overland party into the Arctic. He left Liverpool for Montreal on February 17, 1833, then left for Great Slave Lake, where he established winter quarters at a new outpost he named Fort Reliance. There, on April 25, 1834, Back received the news that Ross had been rescued. He also received new orders to proceed to the shores of the Arctic Ocean and continue the mapping of the coast from Point Turnagain to James Ross's westernmost position.

Back followed the Great Fish (now Back) River north in July 1834 with a twelve-man party. In his journal, he wryly described his progress while standing on the shores of the sea: "This, then, may be considered as the mouth [of the river] . . . which, after a violent and tortuous course of two hundred and thirty geographical miles, running through an iron-ribbed country without a single tree on the whole line of its banks, expanding into fine large lakes with clear horizons, most embarrassing to the navigator, and broken into falls, cascades, and rapids to the

number of no less than eighty-three in the whole, pours its waters into the Polar Sea."

Unable to reach either Point Turnagain or Ross's position, Back turned around on August 16. He noted a strait separating the mainland from "King William Land," but his chart, frustratingly vague, could not connect Point Turnagain with Ross's farthest point, Boothia Felix, or Prince Regent Inlet. A series of lines, some tentative, but separated by blank space, were all that delineated a region we now know to be an intricate part of the Arctic archipelago.

Back returned to England in August 1835 and to an ongoing discussion over whether or not some waterway might connect Prince Regent Inlet and the Gulf of Boothia. James Ross had been told by the Inuit that there was a northern connection just below Cape Garry: this was later proven correct when Bellot Strait was finally charted. John Ross disagreed, while Back argued that there were "strong inferences in favour of a southern channel." Back also felt that Pocte's Bay did not exist and that a channel did run down the eastern shores of "King William Land," although how it connected with the rest of the polar sea was as yet unknown. Back's well-written account of his journey met with much acclaim and inspired a return to the Arctic, this time by sea.

Terror on Repulse Bay, 1836–37

Acting on the recommendations of the Royal Geographical Society, which had supported the search for the Northwest Passage since John Barrow's renewal of the quest in 1818, the Admiralty gave George Back command of the bomb *Terror*. His instructions were to head to Repulse Bay and anchor there or at Wager Bay, then cross the Melville Peninsula and chart the shoreline north to Fury and Hecla Strait, west to the mouth of the Great Fish (Back) River and thence west again to Point Turnagain. He was to accomplish all this in a single season, "escaping from the gloomy and unprofitable waste of eight month's detention."

Terror's crew works to free the ship from the ice.
National Archives of Canada

Sailing from Chatham on June 14, 1836, *Terror* reached Hudson Strait on August 14. Here, off Salisbury Island, Back had to select the route north; not surprisingly, he followed Edward Parry's track through Frozen Strait. Forcing her way through the ice, the ship was finally frozen in on September 20. *Terror* drifted in the open water at the mercy of the sea and the ice, an ordeal that would last for ten months.

In February, the ice shifted and began to squeeze *Terror*. "The ship now began to complain, and strained considerably," Back wrote. "She heeled over to port" so far that the yards brushed against the ice and tore "gaping rents in the snow walls" that surrounded the ship. "All this time the crashing, grinding, and rushing noise beneath, as well as at the borders of floe, the rents and cracks in all directions towards the ship, herself suffering much, [and] the freezing cold of –33

degrees, combined to render our situation not a little perilous and uncomfortable."

When *Terror* broke free on July 13, Back beat a quick retreat. The ship was so strained that he described her as "crazy, broken and leaky," with the men constantly kept at the pumps. On reaching the west coast of Ireland, he ran the sinking *Terror* aground on a sandy beach. The sturdy bomb was repaired, but Back's health was broken and he retired, never again to take to the sea or return to the Arctic.

This failure did not deter one final private expedition, led by two Hudson's Bay Company traders, Peter Dease and Thomas Simpson. Dease had aided Franklin on his second expedition. In 1837, Dease and Simpson journeyed in Franklin's footsteps down the Mackenzie River and then west to Point Barrow, closing the gap left when Franklin and Beechey had been unable

to meet. In 1838–39, they successfully mapped
much of the Arctic coast from the Coppermine
River toward Great Fish (Back) River, keeping
open the question of what lay between it and
Boothia Felix and the true nature of "King William
Land." Dease and Simpson did, however, cross
Coronation Gulf and reach the shores of Victoria
Island. They traced its shoreline to the west as
far as Cambridge Bay, where the prominent land-
mark in the area was named Mount Pelly after
the Governor of the Hudson's Bay Company.

When Barrow assembled the charts and maps
of the Arctic from the various expeditions, they
delineated a more or less charted Arctic coast at
the top of the continent, a vague number of
coastlines and islands charted during Parry's 1819
push west, and a number of possible entrances to
a Northwest Passage to the west of the Melville
and Boothia Peninsulas. A way might be found
through this maze, but British interest in the passage had waned. The next polar endeavour would
be to the south, with James Clark Ross taking the
bombs *Terror* and *Erebus* to Antarctica for three
years of exploration, scientific inquiry and charting between 1839 and 1843. But Ross's southern
voyages reawakened the taste for adventure, and
in 1845, the Admiralty decided to make one last
try for the Northwest Passage.

CHAPTER 6

Franklin Lost, the Passage Discovered

Our Investigator *had the task of bringing Franklin's fate to light; in this she failed; but another task, the object of centuries of endeavour, a task in which many expeditions besides Franklin's had been sacrificed, was fully achieved, so that we now know of not one but two Northwest Passages.* —JOHANN MIERTSCHING, 1854

O VER A TWO-DECADE PERIOD, energetic British probes into the Arctic, both by land and sea, had shown that a Northwest Passage through the ice-filled maze of the Arctic archipelago was possible. Sir John Barrow pointed this out in a letter to the First Lord of the Admiralty in 1844:

> The discovery of Baffin, which pointed out, among others, the great opening of Lancaster on the Western coast of that bay which bears his name, has in our time been found to lead into the Polar Sea through which the North-West Passage from the Atlantic to the Pacific will one day be accomplished, and for the execution of which we are now contending, and which if left to be performed by some other power, England by her neglect of it after having opened the East and West doors should be laughed at by all the world for having hesitated to cross the threshold.

John Franklin's Final Voyage, 1845

Picking up the gauntlet flung down by Barrow, the Lords Commissioners of the Admiralty

decided to dispatch the ships *Erebus* and *Terror*, just back from an Antarctic expedition, into the north. With these seasoned ships, Barrow felt, "there can be no objection with regard to any apprehension of the loss of ships or men."

The Admiralty first offered command of the expedition to Sir James Clark Ross, but he, having promised his wife that he would not sail on any new voyages of exploration, declined. Ross and Parry recommended that the Admiralty give the expedition to Sir John Franklin. Now fifty-nine years of age and considered old by many of his peers, the veteran Arctic explorer was nonetheless a logical choice. Moreover, as Parry told the First Lord of the Admiralty, "He is a fitter man than any I know, and if you don't let him go, the man will die of disappointment."

In February 1845, the Admiralty appointed Franklin to the command of the expedition. His instructions were to proceed through Lancaster Sound and Barrow Strait toward Cape Walker, close to where Parry had been stopped by the ice twenty-five years earlier. He was then to lead either south or north, but always westward, "towards Bering Strait in as straight a line as is permitted by ice or any unknown land." The Royal Navy placed 134 officers and men under Franklin, among them Arctic and Antarctic veteran Captain Francis Rawdon Moira Crozier, commanding HMS *Terror*, and Commander James Fitzjames in charge of HMS *Erebus*.

FACING PAGE This, the only photo (a daguerrotype) of Captain Sir John Franklin, was probably taken aboard HMS *Erebus*, along with portraits of the expedition's officers, just before they sailed, 1845. National Maritime Museum, Greenwich/9191A

BELOW Admiralty model of HMS *Erebus*. The rounded form, bluff bow and sturdy construction seemingly made the ship ideal for Arctic service. In the end, however, she was no match for the relentless ice. National Maritime Museum, Greenwich/D606

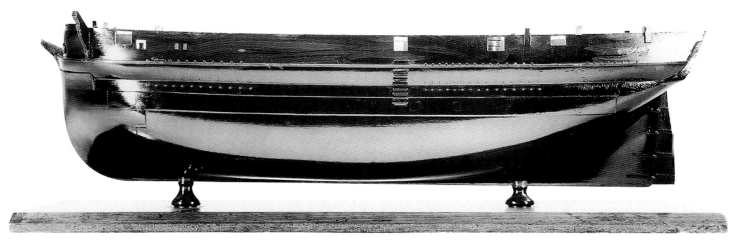

Historian Richard C. Davis sums John Franklin up thus: "The man who charted nearly 1,850 miles of the coastline of North America is best remembered as the leader of an expedition that cost . . . two ships and the lives of 129 men."

John Franklin was a sixty-one-year-old, forty-seven-year veteran of the Royal Navy when he died on his last, ill-fated expedition. Born at Spilsby, England, on April 16, 1786, one of twelve children, Franklin went to sea at age thirteen. A year later he entered the Royal Navy and in 1801 fought at the Battle of Copenhagen. Franklin discovered his calling when he was posted to HMS *Investigator* and learned geography, surveying and charting while mapping the coast of Australia.

The Napoleonic Wars interrupted his surveying career, and he was aboard HMS *Bellerophon* at the Battle of Trafalgar. After serving on HMS *Bedford*, which carried the Portuguese royal family to Brazil as they fled advancing French troops, he fought in the war against the United States.

Franklin returned to exploration and surveying in 1818, when he commanded HMS *Trent* on an attempt on the North Pole from Spitsbergen. Ice turned his ship back, but the fascination of the Arctic had hold of him. In 1819–22, he led a land expedition down the Coppermine River across Canada to the Arctic Ocean, and after his return home married poet Eleanor Porden. They had one child, a daughter. In 1825, he was ordered back to the Arctic and en route learned that his wife had died. His second land expedition took him down the Mackenzie River to the Arctic Ocean. After writing an account of

his journey, he married Jane Griffin, a family friend. He was knighted in 1829 in recognition of his explorations.

From 1829 to 1834, Franklin commanded HMS *Rainbow* in the Mediterranean, then he and Lady Franklin went to Tasmania, where he served as lieutenant-governor between 1837 and 1843. After being recalled to England, he pressed for the opportunity to lead what was envisioned to be the final expedition to search for a Northwest Passage. Franklin sailed with his men into the ice, and history. Not until 1859 did his wife and the world receive definite news of his fate: he had died aboard HMS *Erebus* on June 11, 1847, while his expedition was beset by ice off King William Island.

The two ships were outfitted with steam engines and propellers, and provisioned with supplies for a three-year voyage. Lieutenant Fairholme of *Erebus* wrote home that "Fortnum and Mason [London grocers] have done their part well and we find all of their stores of the best description." The two ships also carried large libraries—in all, 2,900 books—and Fairholme commented: "We find that there is scarcely a book we can think of as being required that is not in the list" of the ships' libraries. Scientific instruments, together with hand organs for musical performances, were also loaded into *Erebus* and *Terror*. "It is curious how few wants we find," Fairholme went on to say. "There is scarcely anything that would be of use that has been neglected and I really do not think that, if I could be in London for an hour or two, I would want to get anything!"

The lieutenant's sentiments were echoed by

Captain F. R. M. Crozier, in command of HMS *Terror*, 1845. National Maritime Museum, Greenwich/91911

Commander James Fitzjames, in command of HMS *Erebus*, 1845. National Maritime Museum, Greenwich/9191B

Erebus and Terror

The two ships selected for the Franklin expedition were veterans of polar exploration and, like many of their predecessors, were originally Royal Navy "bomb vessels." These vessels were specially built stout and wide to absorb the recoil of firing bombs (shells) from the large mortars they carried. The Admiralty thought that their strong construction made them ideal vessels to withstand the ice on polar expeditions and converted several to this use.

Terror was the older of the two. Built at Topsham, England, she was laid down in September 1812 and launched on June 29, 1813. *Terror* was one of three sister ships of the *Vesuvius* class, which also included the bomb *Beelzebub*. *Terror* carried two mortars, ten cannon, and a crew of sixty-seven men.

Erebus was laid down at the Pembroke Dockyard in October 1824 and launched on June 7, 1826, one of the last bombs purpose-built for the Royal Navy. A *Hecla* class vessel, she was one of eight that included two other bombs outfitted for Arctic service, Edward Parry's *Hecla* and *Fury*. *Erebus* carried the same armament as *Terror* and the same number of crew.

Terror had already been employed in two polar expeditions. The first was in 1836, when she was used by George Back during his attempt to reach Repulse Bay. Repaired and refitted, *Terror* accompanied *Erebus* as part of Sir James Clark Ross's Antarctic expedition of 1839–41.

Both vessels were modified extensively for polar service, beginning in 1836 when *Terror* was readied for Back's expedition. The open interior of the ships was filled with a number of cabins. The hull was strengthened with the addition of iron plates over the bow and an extra layer of planking on the sides. The major modification, for the Franklin expedition, was the installation of steam engines and propellers. Railway locomotive engines were used, with that for *Erebus* coming from the London-Greenwich Railway.

Commander Fitzjames, in charge of *Erebus*, wrote to his wife during the refit that "our engine has come alongside. It came drawn by ten coal black horses and weighs fifteen tons."

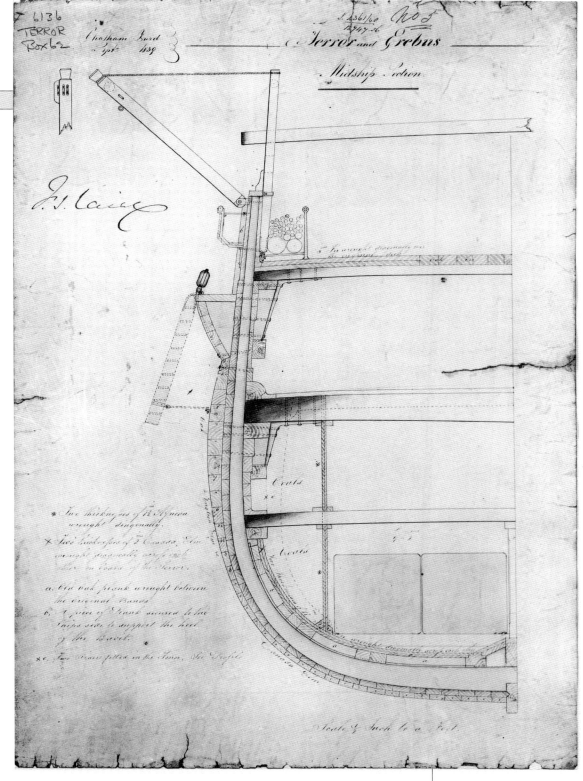

Plan of the hull for *Erebus* and *Terror*, showing how the Royal Navy strengthened them by adding extra planking to the sides and heavy "ice beams" inside. National Maritime Museum Greenwich/6136

Victorians were both horrified and thrilled by the
tragedy of the Franklin expedition, as shown in paintings—
like this imagined scene
titled *They Forged the Last*

Link with Their Lives, by
Thomas Smith—as well as in
poems and songs. National
Maritime Museum, Greenwich/
BH1273

The Times of London in May 1845, as the expedition prepared to depart: "The Lords Commissioners of the Admiralty have, in every respect, provided most liberally for the comforts of the officers and men of an expedition which may, with the facilities of the screw propeller, and other advantages of modern science, be attended with great results." Indeed, it seemed, nothing could go wrong.

On the morning of May 19, 1845, *Erebus* and *Terror* weighed anchor and sailed from the Thames to rendezvous with a supply ship, *Baretto Junior*, off the Greenland coast. There, at Disko harbour, near today's Godhaven, the last supplies were loaded, and the fresh livestock taken aboard in England was slaughtered. Six men were returned as being "unfit." The last letters and journals written by the officers and men on the voyage from England were handed to Lieutenant Edward Griffiths, master of *Baretto Junior*, to take back home. Franklin, writing to Parry, reported that the weather had been fine, adding: "I think it must be favourable for the opening of the ice."

On July 28, *Erebus* and *Terror* reached Baffin Bay, where they encountered the whalers *Enterprise* and *Prince of Wales*. Franklin moored his ships to a large iceberg, waiting for favourable conditions to enter Lancaster Sound. Captain Dannett, who hosted several officers aboard his ship, *Prince of Wales*, commented in his log that "Both ships crews are all well, and in remarkable spirits, expecting to finish the operation in good time." After their brief sojourn with the whalers, *Erebus* and *Terror* continued on to their destiny. The Arctic closed around them, and they vanished.

First Searches by Sea and Land, 1848–50

One of the first to worry about Franklin was John Ross. The experienced explorer knew well enough what hazards the Arctic could bring, having lost *Victory* and endured a long ordeal on the Boothia Peninsula. Ross wrote to the Admiralty in September 1846, informing it of his promise to Franklin that should no report arrive from the expedition by January 1847, he would lead a

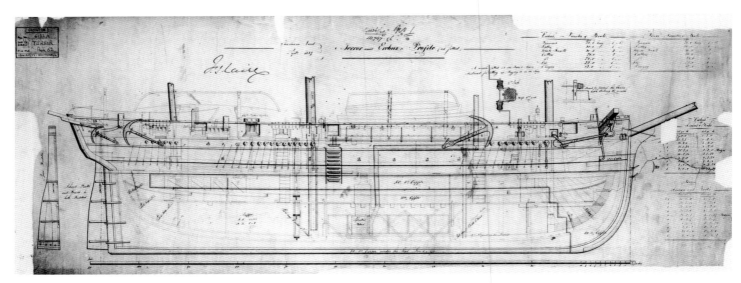

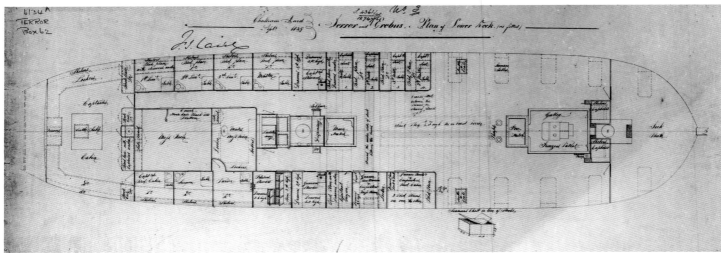

TOP **Profile plan of *Erebus* and *Terror*, as fitted for Arctic service.** National Maritime Museum, Greenwich/6132

BOTTOM **Lower deck plan of *Erebus* and *Terror*, as fitted for Arctic service.** National Maritime Museum, Greenwich/6134

Provisions for an Arctic Voyage

The Admiralty provided the Franklin expedition with an enormous quantity of dried, salted and "preserved" (canned) food. In 1939, Franklin expedition historian R. J. Cyriax calculated the amounts as follows:

biscuit	36,487 lbs.
flour	136,656 lbs.
pemmican	1,203 lbs.
[salt] beef in 8-lb. pieces	32,224 lbs.
[salt] pork in 4-lb. pieces	32,000 lbs.
preserved meat	33,289 lbs.
preserved vegetables	8,900 lbs.
concentrated spirits	3,684 gallons
sugar	23,576 lbs.
wine for the sick	200 gallons
suet	3,052 lbs.
raisins	1,008 lbs.
[dried] peas	147 barrels
chocolate	9,450 lbs.
tea	2,357 lbs.
lemon-juice	9,300 lbs.
concentrated soup	20,463 pints
vinegar	1,326 gallons
scotch barley	2,496 lbs.
oatmeal	1,350 gallons
pickles	580 gallons
cranberries	170 gallons
mustard	1,000 lbs.
pepper	200 lbs.

The salt beef and pork were packed in barrels of thick brine, and were usually soaked for twenty-four hours in water, then boiled. A staple of sailors' diets for centuries, the salt meat could last for years. The dense, unleavened baked biscuit, also known as "hardtack," was another seaman's staple; it too, could last for years. The Vancouver Maritime Museum has in its collections a biscuit from HMS *Fury*, left on the beach in 1825, that technically could still be eaten.

The "pickles" were pickled cabbage, onions and walnuts, and a "mixed" combination.

rescue mission. Also, he pointed out that Franklin "cannot have succeeded in passing through Behring's Straits; because the expedition, had it been successful, would have been heard of before the middle of this month . . . the probability is, that his ships have been carried by drift ice into a position from which they cannot be extricated."

The Admiralty solicited the opinion of several other Arctic veterans, who all agreed that there was as yet no great cause for alarm. The Admiralty also offered a reward for news of Franklin to the whalers working the eastern Arctic. As well, it slowly developed plans for a relief ship or ships to be sent to the eastern and western ends of the Arctic, for it clearly was prudent to watch both sides of the passage. Frederick Beechey pointed out that "The season of 1849 will be one of painful anxiety," because by then Franklin's supplies would have run out.

In 1848, the Admiralty placed James Clark Ross in command of the rescue mission to the eastern Arctic. He was to voyage west through Lancaster Sound in HMS *Enterprise* and HMS *Investigator*, the latter commanded by Captain Edward Joseph Bird. In addition, the Admiralty dispatched HMS *Plover*, in charge of Commander Thomas Edward Laws Moore, and HMS *Herald*, under the command of Captain Henry Kellett, to the western Arctic. After finding a winter harbour, *Plover* was to send out two boats east "along the coast in search of the voyagers." If necessary, *Plover* was to stay two years while *Herald* sailed south to pick up supplies and returned to replenish her.

Both expeditions failed to find any trace of Franklin or his ships. Ross encountered heavy ice and was unable to press far, so *Enterprise* and *Investigator* stopped for the winter at Port Leopold on Somerset Island. He searched both coasts of the island with sledge crews. He also trapped and then released Arctic foxes, after tagging them with specially engraved metal collars in the hope that the message would alert the

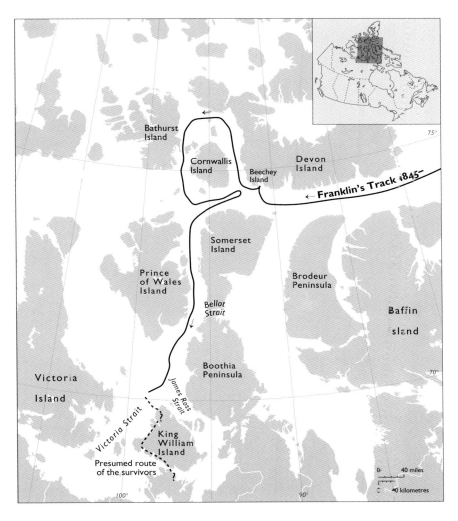

crews of *Erebus* and *Terror* to the presence of rescue ships. But the collars, like the voyage, were a failure. When the ice finally retreated, *Enterprise* and *Investigator* managed to get out of Port Leopold, only to be trapped again by ice. Fortunately, a group of icebergs broke up the field, allowing the ships to pull into open water. Ross decided that they had pushed their luck far enough and returned to England. On the arrival home of *Enterprise* and *Investigator* in November 1849, Ross was in the unfortunate position of having little to add to knowledge of either the Arctic or Franklin's fate. Controversy surrounded his early return, and even though the Admiralty and Lady Franklin both supported Ross's decision, critics dogged him for years afterward.

Meanwhile, the other expedition with *Plover* and *Herald* had also entered the Arctic, but from

the western end. Kellett, in *Herald*, reached Bering Strait first and went through, but a storm drove *Plover* west to Siberia's shores, where she spent the winter of 1848–49. When the ice broke up on June 13, *Plover* headed east across Bering Strait to Kotzebue Sound, where she met up with *Herald* and the private yacht *Nancy Dawson*. The three ships moved east along the Alaskan coast to Wainright Inlet. There, four boats, under the command of Lieutenant W. J. S. Pullen, were detached to journey farther east to look for traces of Franklin. *Nancy Dawson* accompanied the boats as far as Point Barrow before putting back. Pullen and the boats continued on to the mouth of the Mackenzie River, following Franklin's track from his second expedition. Ice, storms and the unwanted attention of Inuit threatened the boats and crews. But Pullen was

ABOVE *Enterprise* and *Investigator* in winter quarters during James Clark Ross's search for Franklin, 1848–49. From W. H. Browne, *Ten Coloured Views*

FACING PAGE Sledge parties from James Clark Ross's *Enterprise* and *Investigator*, searching for traces of Franklin, 1848–49. From W. H. Browne, *Ten Coloured Views*

£20,000
Sterling
(100,000 DOLLARS,)
REWARD.

TO BE GIVEN by her Britannic Majesty's Government to such a private Ship, or distributed among such private Ships, of any Country, as may, in the judgment of the Board of Admiralty, have rendered efficient assistance to

SIR JOHN FRANKLIN,

HIS SHIPS, or their Crews,

and may have contributed directly to extricate them from the Ice.

H. G. WARD,
SECRETARY TO THE ADMIRALTY.

LONDON, 23rd MARCH, 1849.

The attention of WHALERS, or any other Ships disposed to aid in this service, is particularly directed to SMITH'S SOUND and JONES'S SOUND, in BAFFIN'S BAY, to REGENT's INLET and the GULF of BOOTHIA, as well as to any of the Inlets or Channels leading out of BARROW'S STRAIT, or the Sea beyond, either Northward or Southward.

VESSELS Entering through BEHRING'S STRAITS would necessarily direct their search North and South of MELVILLE ISLAND.

NOTE.—Persons desirous of obtaining Information relative to the Missing Expedition, which has not been heard of since JULY, 1845, are referred to EDMUND A. GRATTAN, Esq., Her Britannic Majesty's Consul, BOSTON, MASSACHUSETTS : or, ANTHONY BARCLAY, Esq., Her Majesty's Consul, NEW YORK.

Reward poster for the rescue of Franklin and his crews, 1849. National Maritime Museum, Greenwich/D1056

able to reach the safety of the Hudson's Bay Company's fur-trading outpost of Fort Simpson.

While Pullen and his crew were en route home via Hudson Bay, new orders came to return to the Arctic and proceed north in the boats. Pullen dutifully set out, but once the boats travelled out past the Mackenzie River and into the Arctic Ocean, the early onset of winter and the daunting threat of ice and cold thwarted him. He retreated again to Fort Simpson, and in the spring of 1851 he and his men returned home.

Even as its ships pushed from both east and west, the Admiralty had a third search party, this one by land, on the trail. One of its members was Hudson's Bay Company surgeon and explorer Dr. John Rae.

On his first Arctic expedition, in 1846, Rae had continued the survey of the Arctic coast pursued by Dease and Thomas Simpson in 1837–39. Rae's instructions were simple: "complete the geography of the northern shore of America." After journeying up the west coast of Hudson Bay to Repulse Bay, he had followed the coast west past Committee Bay to Pelly Bay, then the southern end of the Boothia Peninsula, filling in a gap in the map that had existed since John Ross's second expedition. With winter coming on, Rae retreated to Repulse Bay. He and his men built a small stone outpost, which they named Fort Hope, and settled down. In early April 1847, with snow still on the ground, Rae crossed the Melville Peninsula—effectively completing a task originally set for George Lyon's ill-fated *Griper* expedition in 1824 and George Back's aborted, near-disastrous repeat of it in 1836. He stopped just 10 miles short of Fury and Hecla Strait, filling in yet another part of the empty map.

On his return to England to report his findings, Rae was swept up in the first wave of the search for Franklin. While the Admiralty and the HBC were not on the best of terms, the Company provided Rae's services to Sir John Richardson, who planned to follow his and Franklin's old overland track to find some trace of his missing friend. The two men, joined by a group of Royal Navy seamen, searched the Arctic coast to the Coppermine River through 1848. However, as Rae reported, "I am sorry to say that we have been quite unsuccessful in object of our voyage."

The First Trace

The first trace of Franklin came in July 1849, after the relief missions had sailed. A small copper cylinder, one of many with which the Admiralty had equipped the expedition, was picked out of the rocks on the west coast of Greenland. By the time the cylinder was found, with its smudged, blue-streaked form inside, Franklin had been missing for four years.

On every day spent above the Arctic Circle, Franklin was to complete a standard form, place it in a cylinder and throw it into the sea. Printed instructions in English, French, Spanish, Dutch, Danish and German stated: "Whoever finds this paper is requested to forward it to the Secretary of the Admiralty, London, *with a note of the time and place at which it was found*; or, if more conven-ient, to deliver it for that purpose to the British Consul at the nearest port."

Disappointingly, the cylinder came from the start of the expedition and reported that *Erebus*, in consort with *Terror* and *Baretto Junior*, was at 66° north latitude, 54°20' west longitude on June 30, 1845, just ready to cross the Arctic Circle and proceed on to Disko.

Enter the Americans, 1850–51

Anxiety was growing in England, as one member of the House of Commons stated, for "those who were now passing a fifth year—if God should have spared their lives—amid the horrors of an Arctic winter."

Three expeditions left within months of each other in 1850. The first was originally a private effort organized by Lady Jane Franklin, the lost explorer's second wife, who was eager to continue the search. The expedition was formally adopted and outfitted by the Admiralty, and placed under the command of whaling skipper William Penny on the brig *Lady Franklin*, joined

Satirical cartoon showing an icy Britannia "ruling the waves," albeit frozen, during the search for Franklin.
National Library of Canada/ c28274

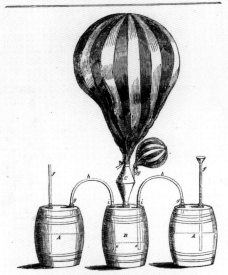

by the brig *Sophia*, in charge of Alexander Stewart. It sailed from Aberdeen, Scotland, in April.

Lady Jane Franklin provided her own money for an expedition commanded by Charles C. Forsyth on the brig *Prince Albert*, which departed from Aberdeen in June, bound for Prince Regent Inlet and the Boothia Peninsula. Yet another private search party was funded by public subscribers, with the Hudson's Bay Company making the largest contribution. This group sponsored the aged Sir John Ross, then seventy-two years old, to once again head into the Arctic. Departing from Loch Ryan, Scotland, in May 1850 in the schooner *Felix*, Ross also took along his own yacht, the 12-ton *Mary*, for use as a tender. All of the ships from the three expeditions were to convene at Barrow Strait to search the surrounding area to the north, south and west.

But the Lords Commissioners of the Admiralty did not place their entire faith in these smaller expeditions. In May 1850, they also dispatched two substantial expeditions, again searching from both east and west. The first was under the overall command of Captain Horatio T. Austin, in HMS *Resolute*, who was to enter the Arctic from the east. He was joined by HMS *Assistance*, under the command of Captain Erasmus Ommaney, and two steam tenders, *Intrepid* commanded by Lieutenant Sherard Osborn and *Pioneer*, by Lieutenant John Bertie Cator. Austin's instructions were to sail west to Melville Island, searching the surrounding coast as he made his way there. The other expedition was to the western Arctic, led by Captain Richard Collinson in *Enterprise*, joined by Commander Robert McClure in charge of *Investigator*.

Lady Franklin had written a letter in 1849 to Zachary Taylor, the President of the United States, asking that an American expedition join the search. "I am not without hope," she stated, "that you will deem it not unworthy of a great and kindred nation to take up the cause of humanity which I plead." Politics bogged down her request, but the intervention of New York shipping merchant Henry Grinnell broke the impasse. He purchased two small brigs, *Advance* and *Rescue*. Congress appropriated funds to outfit the ships, and the U.S. Navy provided the officers and crews to man them. Under the command of Lieutenant Edwin J. DeHaven, the expedition, with DeHaven in *Advance* and Acting Master Samuel P. Griffin in command of *Rescue*, left New York in May 1850.

The Americans joined the British ships in Barrow Strait. Their participation was significant, making the search for Franklin a more international effort. The "First Grinnell Expedition," as it came to be known, was the first official United States expedition into the Arctic, inaugurating a series of later excursions that culminated in Robert Peary's push for the North Pole.

In spite of all the excitement, there was no romance in the quest for Robert Randolph Carter, first officer of *Rescue*. He wrote in his diary that "everyone talks of the Expedition and how much we are to do, all of course certain that we are to find Sir John and the N.W. Passage and return in one season. My reflections are 'with those two little boats just land me safely anywhere in a Christian country after two years of intense suffering, hardship, and disgust, and I will be thankful.'" Carter's uneasiness was well-founded. The perils of the ice were infamous, and the fact that the experienced Franklin, with two well-equipped ships, had vanished in the unforgiving land, underscored the danger.

That summer of 1850, traces of *Erebus* and *Terror* were finally found. Searchers from Horatio Austin's expedition aboard HMS *Assistance* were in the Arctic archipelago, following what they hoped was Franklin's course. They proved to be on the right track. At Cape Riley on Devon Island, they discovered a temporary camp, and Captain Erasmus Ommaney of *Assistance* reported: "I had the satisfaction of meeting with the first traces of Sir John Franklin's expedition, consisting of fragments of naval stores, ragged portions of clothing, preserved meat tins &c."

Lady Jane Franklin

Few figures have loomed so large in the quest for the Northwest Passage as Jane Griffin, Lady Franklin. Her single-minded determination to force the Admiralty to rescue her husband and his stranded crews, and later, when it seemed they were dead, to ascertain their fate, is near legendary.

Jane Griffin, born in 1791, was an intelligent, forthright, determined woman, who at an early age decided that the conventions of ordinary society would not bind her. When only seventeen, she decided to tour a prison ship moored near Plymouth. An active reader, traveller and diarist, she held potential suitors—including Dr. Roget, author of the famous thesaurus—at bay.

Miss Griffin first met John Franklin, who became famous in England as "the man who ate his boots," after he returned from his second Arctic expedition and married her friend, poet Eleanor Porden. Following Eleanor's death and Franklin's return from his third expedition, Jane Griffin married the stolid Franklin in November 1828.

When Franklin sailed on his fourth and final Arctic expedition in 1845, the independent Lady Jane took the opportunity to tour the West Indies and the United States. But when there was no news from her husband, she began a campaign to push the Admiralty into launching a search and rescue expedition. In addition, she spent more than £3,000 of her own money, a considerable sum for its day, purchasing three different vessels and sending four separate expeditions of her own into the Arctic to find her lost husband and his men. As time went by and the situation grew hopeless, she turned her efforts to ensuring that John Franklin's memory and his achievements would be remembered. Due to her efforts, they are not forgotten.

Lady Jane Franklin. Vancouver Maritime Museum

**The ice-clogged straits off
Beechey Island.** George
Hobson

Then, on nearby Beechey Island, they found a tall cairn marking the spot where *Erebus* and *Terror* had wintered during the expedition's first year in the Arctic. Other search ships converged on the site to comb the area for clues. Another temporary campsite was found at Cape Spencer, also on Devon Island, but the majority of relics came from Beechey.

Beechey's shores held the traces of a garden, the rock foundations of three temporary buildings, two cairns and the graves of three of Franklin's crew. One of the cairns was built out of hundreds of empty meat tins, filled with gravel and stacked high. Searchers also found smaller, scattered items and a pair of gloves, set out to dry and weighed down by a rock. A pike pole stuck into the shore, with a small painted hand pointing toward the water, aroused considerable speculation. Was it a marker indicating where the expedition had gone? The searchers concluded it had been set up to guide shore parties back across the snow and ice to *Erebus* and *Terror*.

The three graves, marked by wooden headboards, held the bodies of Royal Marine William Braine of *Erebus*, able seaman John Hartnell, also of *Erebus*, and leading stoker John Torrington of *Terror*. Torrington had been the first member of the expedition to die. His grave was dated January 1, 1846; Hartnell had died on January 4, and Braine on April 3. The three deaths, so close together, seemed unusual. Captain Ommaney, writing home, suggested that the expedition's preserved food was "of an inferior quality."

Three out of 129 men were now accounted for. But where was the rest of the vanished expedition—the ships, the men?

From Beechey Island, the trail turned cold. The ships separated to search different areas and to assess the claim of Inuit interpreter Adam Beck that a group of white sailors had been massacred at a placed called Omaneq. Ice prevented the searchers from sailing west to Melville Island, and when winter came on, Austin found himself and his four ships frozen in off Griffith Island, near modern Resolute. Forsyth returned home after a brief survey in the area of Fury Beach, while the Penny and Ross expeditions wintered at Assistance Harbour.

The two American ships, not as prepared for Arctic conditions as their more experienced British counterparts, had orders to return before the winter. However, they were caught in the ice and drifted 60 miles up Wellington Channel, between Devon and Cornwallis Islands, before the ice shifted and they drifted back out. A sledge party, led by Penny, also penetrated Wellington Channel during the winter. Both forays into the channel followed what was later determined to be part of Franklin's route and mapped new areas, including the Grinnell Peninsula, which was a portion of Devon Island named for the American patron who had purchased *Advance* and *Rescue*.

The British in particular spent the winter probing west, south and north on sledge journeys. Among the most energetic explorers was a young lieutenant, Francis Leopold McClintock. He sledged all the way to Parry's farthest western point of Melville Island and left a record of his visit at Winter Harbour before returning to his ship. On the eighty-day trip, he and his crew trekked 770 miles.

Meanwhile, Ommaney, Osborn and two of their officers, unwittingly on Franklin's track, reached Cape Walker, which they discovered was part of an island. Beyond it was another, larger island. This newly discovered land, Prince of Wales Island, was separated from Somerset Island by a narrow passage, Peel Strait. The sledge crews searched along both the west and east shores of Prince of Wales for a trace of Franklin. *Erebus* and *Terror* had in fact passed this way, though the searchers did not know it. More of the Arctic archipelago was charted, filling in gaps in the Admiralty's maps and replacing the surveys doubtless made by Franklin and lost with him.

The Americans spent several harrowing months in their ships *Advance* and *Rescue*, drifting

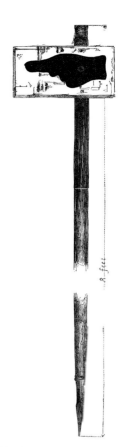

Direction post left by the Franklin expedition on Beechey Island. From *The Illustrated London News*, 4 October 1851

Sledge Travel

Most of the actual work of searching for Franklin was not done by ships. Rather, the ships were usually anchored or frozen in to serve as stationary depots for sledge parties that set out to scour the surrounding region. Some of the sledge journeys were epic; Leopold McClintock's eighty-day journey to Edward Parry's Winter Harbour and back in 1851 was a 770-mile round trip.

Peter Sutherland, surgeon with William Penny's 1850 expedition in search of John Franklin, described in his journal the loading of the 12-foot-long wooden sledges that the men hauled over the snow and ice. In addition to tents, tent poles, ice chisels, pickaxes, ammunition, guns, cooking implements and "fat for fuel," each sledge was "provisioned for forty days . . . the daily allowances per man were pork ¾ lb., pemmican ¾ lb., bread 1 lb., tea ¾ oz., sugar 1 oz., rum 1.2 gill, and tobacco ½ oz." Each sledge when loaded weighed 592 pounds, and was hauled by seven men.

In this arduous fashion, British sailors mapped the Arctic and "discovered" the last gaps of the Northwest Passage.

Sledge party desperately pulling sledge out of a water gap. From *The Arctic World*

east in the icepack. More than once they feared their two small brigs would be crushed. After drifting out of Wellington Channel and into Lancaster Sound, then back into Baffin Bay, they were released from the ice off Greenland in June 1851. After a brief stop, DeHaven re-entered the ice and struggled to sail west, but by mid-August it was obvious *Advance* and *Rescue* would not reach Lancaster Sound, and the order was given to come about and head for home. Robert Randolph Carter noted the decision in his dairy: "So good-bye Sir John, the Yankees have failed to aid you and can only pray for you. God Almighty aid you to escape from what by this time must be an awful position, if any of your party are still in the hands of Arctic deities."

The British expeditions, too, turned for home. Ross left his yacht *Mary* on the shores of Beechey, in the hope it would aid Franklin or other stranded explorers in the future. When the searchers reached Britain in 1851, they faced a disappointed if not angry Admiralty and public. A Committee of Inquiry exonerated and praised Austin and Penny, the leaders of the two official expeditions, concluding, wrongly, that Franklin had not headed south, as the waters off Prince of Wales were considered to be too shallow and ice-clogged for *Erebus* and *Terror* to have passed. Now it was thought that perhaps Franklin had travelled north, through Wellington Channel, and perished there with his crew.

Dr. John Rae: Tales of Disaster and Cannibalism, 1851–54

In 1851, Dr. John Rae was detached from the Hudson's Bay Company for a second time to search for Franklin as well as to chart more of the Arctic coast. After descending the Coppermine River, he crossed Coronation Gulf to "Wollaston Land," which he found was part of Victoria Island. Rae followed the island's west coast to Prince Albert Sound, then turned around and retraced Dease and Simpson's old route along the southern shore. Passing Cambridge Bay, he headed east, then north up the eastern shore of the island.

Mast, often thought to be from Sir John Ross's yacht *Mary*, left on Beechey Island in 1851. George Hobson

Franklin's Medal

The medal appears as a dim image, hanging from his neck in the last daguerreotype of Franklin, taken aboard *Erebus* on the eve of departure. He was proud of this reward from his King, this brightly coloured badge of a Knight Commander of the Royal Hanoverian Guelphic Order. While commanding HMS *Rainbow* in the Mediterranean, Franklin had aided the Greek government, and for his services received from King Otto of Greece the Cross of the Order of the Redeemer. On January 25, 1846, King William IV followed suit with the Guelphic Order medal.

Was this medal buried with him in the Arctic when he died in 1847? Or did his crew, as they marched in their final, fatal retreat, carry it with them in the hope of returning it to his widow? Hudson's Bay Company explorer and trader John Rae acquired the medal from a group of Inuit, probably at Repulse Bay between May 26 and August 4, 1854. Returned to England, it was one of the first tangible pieces of evidence of Franklin's fate.

Sir John Franklin's medal.
National Maritime Museum, Greenwich

On this trek, Rae found a piece of a flagstaff, marked with the Royal Navy's broad arrow, and a piece of oak that most probably came from *Erebus* and *Terror*, which had been trapped in the ice just to the east. But Rae did not realize the significance of these discoveries and reported he had failed to find Franklin. He had, however, added more to the map, and demonstrated remarkable effectiveness as an explorer. Admired by the Inuit, who named him Aglooka (he who takes long strides), Rae had traversed 1,060 miles in thirty-nine days—an amazing feat for Arctic travel.

Rae returned to the Arctic in 1853 to continue his search for Franklin. He set out from Repulse Bay in March 1854, following his old track along the southern shore of the Gulf of Boothia to the southern end of the Boothia Peninsula. Some argument still existed over whether or not the peninsula was an island, and Rae's earlier expedition had not completely resolved the matter. He now definitely showed that Boothia was a peninsula. Trekking farther west, Rae followed the eastern shore of present-day Ross and Rae Straits to join his discoveries with those of Simpson and Dease at Cape Britannia. This proved that despite James Ross's earlier assumption that "King William Land" was a peninsula, it was actually an island. With the gap between Franklin's Point Turnagain and Parry's sighting of Fury and Hecla Strait *terra incognita* filled, the last pieces of the puzzle that had eluded the Admiralty since 1824 had now been put in place, thanks almost entirely to the men of the Hudson's Bay Company, primarily Rae.

From some Inuit, Rae learned that they had seen "about forty men . . . travelling in company southward over the ice, and dragging a boat and sledges with them" on the western shore of King William Island. The Inuit, through sign language, learned that the men's "ship or ships had been crushed by ice, and they were then going to where they expected to find deer to shoot. From the appearance of the men—all of whom, with the exception of an officer, were hauling on the drag-ropes of the sledge, and were looking thin—they were then supposed to be getting short of provisions. . . . the officer was described as being a tall, stout, middle-aged man."

Rae estimated that this meeting had taken place around the winter of 1850. Later that same season, a group of Inuit had found the corpses of some thirty men, as well as graves "about a long day's journey to the north-west of the mouth of a large stream, which can be no other than Back's Great Fish River. . . . Some of the bodies were in a tent or tents; others were under the boat, which had been turned over to form a shelter; and some lay scattered about in different directions. . . . it was supposed that one was that of an officer (chief) as he had a telescope strapped over his shoulders, and his double-barrelled gun lay underneath him." Then, in words that shocked and horrified readers back in Victorian Britain, Rae went on to report that "from the mutilated state of many of the bodies, and the contents of the kettles, it is evident that our wretched countrymen had been driven to the last dread alternative as a means of sustaining life."

That the Inuit reports were about the men from the lost Franklin expedition was beyond doubt. Rae purchased a number of relics that the Inuit had collected from the bodies, including silverware marked with the initials of Franklin, Crozier and ten other officers from *Erebus* and *Terror*, as well as a small circular silver plate engraved with Franklin's name and one of Franklin's medals, his Guelphic Order of Hanover. Other items bearing the names of the lost included a fragment of an undervest marked "F.D.V. 6.1845" (Charles Frederick Des Voeux, lieutenant and mate aboard *Erebus*); an engraved part of a gold watch belonging to James Reid, ice-master on *Erebus*; a knife handle marked with the initials and last name of Cornelius Hickey, a caulker's mate on *Terror*, and a seaman's certificate case marked "W M" that may have belonged to William Mark, an able seaman on *Erebus*.

Portrait of Captain Robert McClure, discoverer of "a Northwest Passage," painted by Stephen Pearce, 1855. National Portrait Gallery, London

From Rae's reports and the relics he sent back to England, it appeared that the Franklin expedition had trekked south from Beechey Island and, somewhere in the vicinity of King William Island, had met with disaster. Many Britons, however, including Lady Franklin, chose to not believe Rae's account of cannibalism and encouraged other searchers to seek further evidence.

The Passage Found: Robert McClure and Richard Collinson, 1850–55

While Austin, Forsyth, Ross, Penny and the Americans who had rendezvoused at Barrow Strait in the eastern Arctic found traces of Franklin, as did Rae's expeditions, the two ships sent by the Admiralty to the western Arctic in 1850, as part of its push from both directions, were also proving themselves.

Captain Richard Collinson, in *Enterprise*, led the expedition, and Commander Robert

Investigator during McClure's voice. From S. Gurney Cresswell, *Dedicated . . . a Series of Eight Sketches in Colour*

McClure, formerly one of Ross's lieutenants, was in charge of *Investigator*. Their orders were to search for Franklin and to finish charting the Arctic coast, approaching from the west through Bering Strait. Both ships departed from England on January 20, 1850, but quickly separated, as *Investigator* was a slow sailer. The two ships reunited in the Straits of Magellan, but once out in the open Pacific and en route to Hawaii for provisions, they again parted ways.

Arriving at Honolulu at the end of June, McClure learned that Collinson and *Enterprise* had departed the day before for Bering Strait. There, *Enterprise* and *Investigator* were to rendezvous with *Plover* and *Herald* for supplies before heading into the Arctic archipelago. McClure, an ambitious man, feared that he and his ship would be left behind by Collinson, perhaps even left on station in the western Arctic. Quickly reprovisioning, McClure departed on July 4. An American whaling captain advised McClure to go through the Aleutians rather than around them, as Collinson was bound to do. By tacking through the rocky, fog-bound islands, McClure risked shipwreck, but he also stood a chance to catch up with and perhaps pass *Enterprise*.

Investigator was nearly wrecked. After passing through the Aleutians, she threaded Bering Strait past the Diomede Islands in a thick fog. McClure later reported that visibility was down to 400 yards, a strong current was running, breakers were roaring so loudly that the men on deck had to shout to be heard by each other, and "the deep sea lead showed that the ship was sweeping over twenty-two fathoms' water only." But the gamble paid off. When *Investigator* met up with *Plover* and *Herald* at the end of July, there was no news of Collinson. Instead of waiting for his superior officer, McClure decided to push on, telling the commanders of the two supply ships that he was convinced *Enterprise* had passed them all in the fog and was now ahead—which was not likely.

Captain Kellett of *Herald* asked McClure to wait twenty-four hours for Collinson. In response,

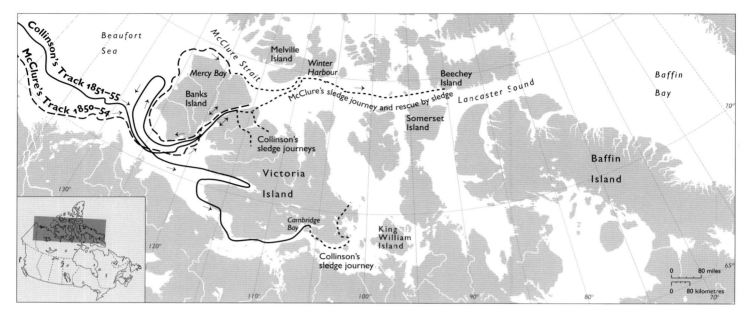

McClure signalled: "Important Duty. Cannot on
my own responsibility." Rather than order him
to wait, Kellett asked McClure to repeat the
signal, which he did, leaving an astounded and
irritated Kellett behind. It would be the last
communication from the headstrong McClure
for years.

Sailing east, McClure followed the Alaskan
coast past Point Barrow, and thence past the
mouth of the Mackenzie River. Nearly halfway
between the Mackenzie and the mouth of the
Coppermine, he headed northeast, landing at the
southern tip of Banks Island. McClure was now
in waters never before visited by a European
vessel. As *Investigator* went up Prince of Wales
Strait, between Banks and Victoria Islands, both
captain and crew noticed that the ice was beginning to thicken. They worried that they were
travelling up an inlet or a dead end. On September 9, McClure surveyed his position and discovered that the ship was only 60 miles from
Barrow Strait. If the water remained open, and if
Investigator was following a strait, then "I cannot
describe my anxious feelings," wrote McClure.
"Can it be possible that this water . . . shall prove
to be the long-sought Northwest Passage? Can it
be that so humble a creature as I am will be per-

mitted to perform what has baffled the talented
and wise for hundreds of years!"

Within a few days, the ship was only 30 miles
from Barrow Strait. But the ice was advancing,
and McClure had to decide whether to turn
around and find a safe harbour for the winter, or
stay frozen in with the ice pack and drift. He
chose to drift, a dangerous option. The ice drove
Investigator back down Prince of Wales Strait, and
the ship was almost lost before the ice froze
solid. Over the winter, small parties set out to
explore the surrounding country. By the end of
October, they had reached the northern end of
the strait and realized, as ship's interpreter
Johann Miertsching wrote in his diary, that they
stood "at the east end of the land Captain Parry
had sighted thirty years before from Melville
Island . . . so the problem of the Northwest
Passage, disputed for 300 years, was solved."

For the rest of the winter, McClure sent out
parties to scout the land for some trace of
Franklin. Instead, they encountered Inuit who
had never before seen Europeans. When the ice
released *Investigator* in August 1851, McClure
decided to try for the passage by going around
the west side of Banks Island. Winter was already
coming on, however, and he feared being caught

**"First Discovery of Land by
H.M.S. Investigator."** From S.
Gurney Cresswell, *Dedicated . . .
a Series of Eight Sketches in Colour*

in the ice. He decided to winter in a sheltered harbour, which he named Mercy Bay, on the north end of the island. It was a decision he would regret; the ice never retreated, and McClure and his crew endured two more years in the Arctic, trapped in Mercy Bay.

By 1852, with no news of *Investigator*, the Admiralty discussed plans to search for the ship and its crew. McClure, meanwhile, was fighting a losing battle with scurvy and the ice. Sledge parties from the ship reached Winter Harbour on Melville Island in mid-1852, but there was no rescue ship waiting to greet them. The ice had prevented any of the other Franklin search vessels from sailing so far west. McClure was filled with despair. Rations were running low, and one of his officers had gone mad and was tied to his bunk. The crew was restless and begging for food. Unless the ship was abandoned soon, the men might not have the strength to march to safety. Even then, it was desperate, and probably a fatal move, as Miertsching wrote in his diary: "When I contemplate the proposed journey, its difficulty, and ourselves . . . there is not the faintest possibility that any one of us should reach England."

In early April 1853, the first member of McClure's crew died, and plans were made to quit *Investigator* on the fifteenth. Then, on the sixth, a solitary figure approached the ship. Heavily bundled, his face blackened by the soot from his coal-oil lamp, he was greeted by McClure: "In the name of God, who are you?" The stranger answered, "I am Lieutenant Pim, late of the *Herald*, and now in the *Resolute*. Captain Kellett is in her at Dealy Island." A note left by McClure at Winter Harbour had guided Pim to the stranded *Investigator*. McClure sledged to *Resolute* with Pim, and agreed with Kellett to abandon ship and return home. On June 3, 1853, three years into his voyage, McClure hoisted the flag, locked the cabin doors and left the ship. For years thereafter, perhaps even decades, the stranded hulk was a boon for wandering groups of Inuit who salvaged wood, metal and supplies.

"The Critical Position of H.M.S. Investigator on the North Coast of Baring Island." From S. Gurney Cresswell, *Dedicated . . . a Series of Eight Sketches in Colour*

"H.M.S. Investigator Running Through a Narrow Channel in a Snow Storm, Between Grounded and Packed Ice."
From S. Gurney Cresswell, *Dedicated . . . a Series of Eight Sketches in Colour*

Upon their return to England in 1854, McClure and his crew were rewarded for the discovery of "a Northwest Passage." They were credited with "a passage" because Collinson, who got back in 1855, had also discovered one, even if it was the same one seen by Rae just before him.

Collinson, who arrived in the Arctic after McClure, decided it was too late in the season and retreated. Far more cautious than the overly ambitious, risk-taking McClure, Collinson wintered in Hong Kong and entered the Arctic in 1851, following McClure's track into Prince of Wales Strait. Like McClure, Collinson realized his proximity to Winter Harbour and that a passage existed. He wintered near the end of the strait and sent a sledge party across the ice-clogged water to Winter Harbour. Had they journeyed farther west, *Enterprise*'s men would have discovered the hopelessly trapped *Investigator*.

When the ice began to melt in the summer of 1852, Collinson, instead of sailing around the west side of Banks Island, turned *Enterprise* in the opposite direction, heading east into Coronation Gulf and Dease Strait. The ship was in familiar waters, and at the end of September entered Cambridge Bay, where she wintered. In the spring, sledge parties followed the coast of Victoria Island east. They observed that this was another passage; what they did not realize was that they were very just 40 miles from the last position of Franklin's frozen ships. Nor did they realize they were simply retracing most of Rae's footsteps. A piece of wreckage that Collinson's men discovered on the island's shores was doubtless a "relic" of Franklin, but they did not journey east across the ice toward King William Island, as there was no clue to induce them to do so.

Collinson's voyage showed that a large ship could sail into the Arctic, from west to east, by following the coast, but his achievement was marred by his failure to push just a little more. If McClure was too eager, then perhaps Collinson was too timid. Had Collinson not retreated from the Arctic that first winter, he would have caught up with McClure. Had he and his crews advanced farther east, they would have discovered the fate of Franklin.

Still, McClure and Collinson had succeeded in closing the remaining gap to finally prove the existence of two separate Northwest Passages.

Edward Belcher's "Arctic Squadron," 1852–54

While Collinson and McClure were still in the Arctic, the last wave of searchers set out. One was another expedition of Lady Franklin's, which left in June 1851 under the command of William Kennedy in the small *Prince Albert*, with a young French naval sub-lieutenant, Joseph René Bellot, as his second-in-command. In July, Kennedy and Bellot fell in with the Americans in *Advance* and *Rescue* in Baffin Bay. After parting company, Kennedy worked *Prince Albert* down to a winter harbour on Somerset Island. Sledge parties jour-

Winter life aboard Elisha Kent Kane's ship, *Advance*, 1853–54. From Kane, *Arctic Explorations*

neyed down the island's eastern shore past Fury Beach to discover what the Rosses had missed on their desperate race for life in 1833—the narrow strait that separated Somerset Island from the Boothia Peninsula. The strait now bears Bellot's name, conferred after the plucky French lieutenant fell off the ice and drowned while carrying dispatches.

The Americans returned to the Arctic in 1853. Elisha Kent Kane, DeHaven's surgeon on the first expedition, was placed in command, this time in *Advance* alone. He set out at the end of May, with orders to try for "the highest penetrable point of Baffin's Bay." Kane, like other searchers, mistakenly believed that Franklin had headed north. Voyaging well up the Greenland coast to 78°43' north, *Advance* froze into a winter harbour that proved to be a trap. By the summer of 1854, the small brig was still "immovably frozen in, with nine feet of solid ice under her bows." Three men had died, and so Kane, with the other weakened survivors, left the ship and marched south, barely

ABOVE Likeness of Elisha Kent Kane, one of the American searchers for Franklin.
From Kane, *Arctic Explorations*

BELOW Kane's ship *Advance* trapped by the ice, 1853-54.
From Kane, *Arctic Explorations*

The desperate trek of Kane's crew after abandoning their ice-trapped ship, summer 1854. From Kane, *Arctic Explorations*

reaching safety at the Danish settlement of Upernavik in August. The ice claimed the tiny *Advance* and no trace of her was ever found.

But still more casualties and the last Arctic disaster came with the Admiralty's final Franklin search expedition. In 1852, a substantial force of 222 men on five ships— HMS *Resolute* and HMS *Assistance*, the steamers *Pioneer* and *Intrepid*, and the depot ship *North Star*—were placed under the command of Captain Sir Edward Belcher. Belcher, a competent but unpopular officer, had orders to sail north up Wellington Channel to see if Franklin had gone that way. He was also to send two ships, if he could, to Winter Harbour, to look for the missing McClure and Collinson.

Once Belcher's "Arctic Squadron" reached Beechey Island, in mid-August, he split his forces,

as ordered. *North Star* anchored off Beechey to serve as a floating refuge, while *Resolute* and *Intrepid* headed west toward Melville Island. Belcher, with *Assistance* and *Pioneer*, sailed north up Wellington Channel.

On the way, *Resolute* was caught by the ice and nearly wrecked. Her sailing master, George F. McDougall, reported that the edge of the ice "took the ship under the lee gangway, shaking her throughout. A moment had scarcely elapsed ere we became sensible of the ship's lifting, and instinctively each man grasped a rope. . . . Yielding inch by inch before such a powerful lever, the ship at length rested on her keel, but it was but momentary, for in a second she was thrown over on her starboard side . . . the very topmasts bent like whalebone, bringing a fearful

Sir Edward Belcher

Sir Edward Belcher's family had strong associations with Canada. Grandson of William Belcher, governor of the colony of Nova Scotia, Edward was born in Halifax in 1799 and entered the Royal Navy in 1812.

Belcher's first assignment in Arctic waters came in 1826–28, when he was attached to Captain William Frederick Beechey's expedi-tion aboard HMS *Blossom*. After a long career survey-ing coasts around the world, Belcher seemingly retired. A contentious nature and disputes with subordinates did not help his reputation.

When Belcher was called to command the "Arctic Squadron," his difficult per-sonality did not stand in the way. But on that expedi-tion, his reputation was tar-nished when he abandoned four of his ships, although his actions were justified by a court martial.

Belcher published his journals as *The Last of the Arctic Voyages* in 1855 and was appointed, after his retirement, to admiral in 1872. He died in 1877.

Sir Edward Belcher's pro-tractor, used during his Arctic voyage of 1852–54 in search of the Franklin expe-dition. Vancouver Maritime Museum/Michael Paris

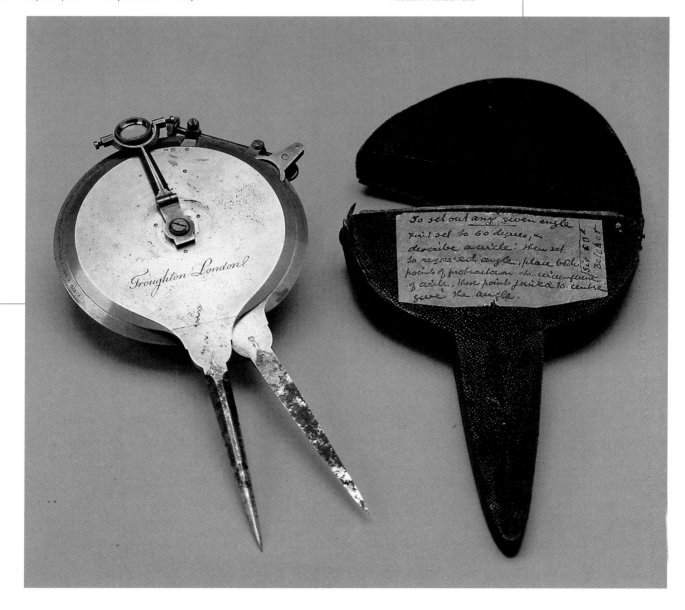

TOP Sir Edward Belcher's "Arctic Squadron" sails from England, in April 1852, to search for the Franklin expedition. From Belcher, *The Last of the Arctic Voyages*

BOTTOM Beechey Island from Devon Island, as well as the narrow isthmus between the two. Owen Beattie

strain." Fortunately, the wind shifted and the ice backed off. At high tide, *Intrepid* managed to pull *Resolute* free.

In early September, *Resolute* and *Intrepid* reached Parry's old Winter Harbour. They were the first ships to anchor there since 1820. When they found McClure's note, plans were made to reach the stranded *Investigator*. Following McClure's rescue in April 1853, sledge parties from the ships surveyed the shores of the surrounding islands, reconfirming Parry's charts and adding new details to the map of the Arctic archipelago. On this epic journey, the dauntless Leopold McClintock proved to be a master of Arctic sledge travel, covering 1,328 miles and charting 886 miles of coastline.

Belcher, meanwhile, with *Assistance* and *Pioneer*, wintered off the Grinnell Peninsula. Sledge trips explored the surrounding area, including a waterway (named Belcher Channel) that separated the peninsula from newly found Cornwall Island. The men from both ships mapped hundreds of miles of coast. Their surveys indicated that no navigable passage existed in this newly charted region to the north and that Franklin's ships had probably not travelled this way.

The expedition's attempts to leave the Arctic in 1853 were prevented by the ice. Belcher, whose coarse, bullying manner infuriated his junior officers, faced growing dissension. As a result, in the spring of 1854, Belcher decided to abandon his ships and return home in the small *North Star*. The commanders of the other ships, particularly Henry Kellett, were appalled, but when Belcher issued a written order for abandonment, the crews of *Resolute*, *Intrepid*, *Assistance*, *Pioneer* and the already abandoned *Investigator* trekked to Beechey Island. There, Commander W. J. S. Pullen, *North Star*'s captain, had built a substantial wooden shore depot, which he named Northumberland House. Supplies from *North Star* and some newly arrived transport ships (*Breadalbane, Talbot* and *Phoenix*) filled the depot, and so the advent of nearly two hundred more

Sledging party of the Belcher expedition departing to search for traces of Franklin and his men. From Belcher, *The Last of the Arctic Voyages*

TOP Winter atmospherics at the winter quarters of the Belcher expedition on Northumberland Sound. From Belcher, *The Last of the Arctic Voyages*

BOTTOM Winter quarters of the Belcher expedition. The ships were banked with ice to insulate them. From Belcher, *The Last of the Arctic Voyages*

men did not strain resources. Even the loss of *Breadalbane*, crushed by the ice and sunk off Beechey, did not pose a threat.

Belcher's expedition crowded into *North Star*, *Talbot* and the steamer *Phoenix*, clearing Beechey Island on August 27, 1854. On their arrival home, Belcher and his officers faced a court-martial over the abandonment of their ships. The responsibility ultimately rested on Belcher's shoulders. Although acquitted, his actions were frowned upon by the Admiralty. The wisdom of abandoning the ships has been the subject of debate ever since, fuelled by the discovery of *Resolute* in the North Atlantic.

TOP Marker for cache left on Dealy Island in 1853 by Captain Henry Kellett of H MS *Resolute*, part of the Belcher expedition, on the Admiralty's final search for Franklin. Vancouver Maritime Museum/St. Roch National Historic Site Collection/HNSO-40-03a

BOTTOM In 1944, the crew of the RCMP schooner *St. Roch* visited the remains of the cache left on Dealy Island in 1853 by Captain Henry Kellett during the Belcher expedition's search for Franklin. Vancouver Maritime Museum/St. Roch National Historic Site Collection/HNSO-40-03a

TOP Kellett's storehouse. He built a substantial stone building, covered with a timber and canvas roof, to protect his cache of food and supplies. M. Bertulli

BOTTOM LEFT On Beechey Island, the Belcher Monument, raised in honour of those who died searching for **Franklin.** George Hobson

BOTTOM RIGHT Monument and ruins of Northumberland House on Beechey Island, the wooden shore depot built by Commander **W. J. S. Pullen of Sir Edward Belcher's "Arctic Squadron," 1852–54.** Stephen Loring

Breadalbane

The northernmost ship-
wreck yet discovered, the
intact hulk of the transport
Breadalbane lies off the
shores of Beechey Island.

Launched in Glasgow,
Scotland, in 1843, the three-
masted bark was a solidly
built 428-ton merchantman
125 feet long, with a 24-foot
beam and an 18-foot depth
of hold. The Admiralty
hired *Breadalbane* to carry
supplies to Beechey Island
to support Sir Edward
Belcher's expedition. Sailing
from Sheerness on May 19,
1853, under the command of
Captain John MacKenzie,
Breadalbane was packed
with a cargo of food, clothing, rum and coal.

Arriving off Beechey on
August 8, 1853, *Breadalbane*

lay to while her crew
unloaded cargo at nearby
Cape Riley, as ice prevented
the transport from reaching
the ships anchored nearby
and discharging her cargo
directly into their holds.

After days of constant
squeezing, overlaid by the
sounds of rumbles and
shrieks as the ice ground
against itself and the ship,
Breadalbane sank when a
floe punched into the hull in
the early morning hours of
August 22.

A nearby observer,
Commander Augustus
Inglefield, wrote that the ice
"passed through her star-
board bow, and in less than
fifteen minutes she sunk in
thirty fathoms of water, giving the people barely

enough time to save them-
selves, and leaving the
wreck of the boat only to
mark the spot where the ice
had closed over her."

On board *Breadalbane*,
second master William
Fawckner, the Royal Navy's
representative and the ship's
second master, was awak-
ened when the pressure
popped open his cabin door.
Rushing below, Fawckner
"roared like a bull to those
in bed to jump out and save
their lives." Every hand
reached the ice safely and
watched as the ship cracked
up "like matches would in
the hand."

The wreck was discov-
ered in August 1980 by a
team assembled by Toronto
physician and diver Joe

MacInnis, working aboard
the Canadian icebreaker
John A. Macdonald.
Subsequent expeditions
photographed the ship and
recovered the wheel, which
currently rests in a refriger-
ated water bath at the
Canadian Conservation
Institute in Ottawa.

Lying in the darkness on
a soft mud bottom 100
metres (320 feet) beneath
the surface of the Arctic
Ocean, *Breadalbane* is a
picture-perfect shipwreck;
intact, with two of her three
masts rising toward the
surface. The third mast lies
on the bottom, close to
where it fell out of the sinking bark. The hole in the
side of the hull that sank the
ship provides a glimpse into

the hold. The cabin still
stands on the deck, and on
a rack, near the bulkhead of
the cabin, is a cabinet, now
gaping open, with compass,
signal lantern and other
instruments ready for the
long-gone helmsman to
consult. *Breadalbane* is truly
a moment frozen in time.

ABOVE The loss of
***Breadalbane*, crushed by ice
off Beechey Island, 1854.**
National Maritime Museum,
Greenwich/c7779

The President's Desk

When the whaler *George Henry* fell in with the derelict *Resolute* on September 10, 1855, she was drifting in the ice a thousand miles distant from where she had been abandoned. After following *Resolute* for six days, Captain Buddington ordered George Tyson and some other men to cross the ice on foot and board her. Tyson reported that the ship was "in a deplorable state. The water-tanks had burst, and the hold was full of water, whilst all perishable items were almost entirely destroyed by cold and damp. Scarcely anything on board, save the salt provisions in casks, and preserved meats in hermetically sealed tins . . . had . . . suffered from the intense hyperborean frost." And yet, while everything "presented a mouldy appearance," the table still held wine decanters and half-filled glasses of wine. Tyson took a sip, and then raised a toast with his

mates to the late officers and crew of *Resolute*.

Captain Buddington decided to rescue the derelict—she would fetch a valuable sum as a salvage prize. With eleven of his crew, he sailed *Resolute* to the United States, leaving his mate in command of *George Henry*.

News of the recovery of *Resolute* astounded both sides of the Atlantic. The Admiralty relinquished all claim to the vessel, and the Congress of the United States bought her. The U.S. Navy refitted the ship "with such care and attention," wrote her former master, George F. MacDougall, "that not only had the ship's stores, even to flags, been replaced, but even the officer's libraries, musical boxes, pictures &c. had been preserved, and . . . restored to their original positions."

Resolute was presented to Queen Victoria in Decem-

ber 1856 as a gesture of goodwill by the American people. The gift was warmly received, but *Resolute* never returned to service and was finally broken up in 1878. The queen, however, sentimental and wishing to reciprocate the gesture, had some of the timbers salvaged and a large, 1,300-pound oak desk made from them. The desk arrived without fanfare—or warning—at the White House on November 23, 1880, with a brass plaque attached to it explaining its history and noting the desk "is presented by the Queen . . . to the President of the United States, as a memorial of the courtesy and loving kindness which dictated the offer of the gift of the *Resolute*."

The desk was used by President Rutherford B. Hayes almost immediately in the White House library. After a long career of use in various rooms, the desk was rescued by First Lady

Jacqueline Kennedy and restored for President John F. Kennedy's use in the Oval Office. One of the most famous photos of President Kennedy shows him at his desk while his young son, John Jr., plays under it. The desk has also been used by Presidents Jimmy Carter, Ronald Reagan, George W. Bush and Bill Clinton.

In August 1855, the steam whaler *Tays* encountered ship wreckage in Davis Strait, "at Latitude 70." The captain reported that "he found part of a steamer's topmast embedded in heavy ice; he also saw the moulded form of a ship's side, and thinks the latter must have sunk." Two weeks later, and 250 miles south, the whaler *George Henry* fell in with the abandoned *Resolute*, still afloat and intact. Some of the whaler's crew sailed *Resolute* to the United States, where she was repaired and returned to England. It underscored the feeling of many that Belcher had prematurely and unwisely left his ships to the ice.

As the years passed, it became obvious that there was no hope of rescuing Franklin and his men. They must be dead, and *Erebus* and *Terror* had probably been crushed by ice and sunk. By the time the search for Franklin ended, the

numerous expeditions, probing into the Arctic from both east and west, had completed much of the mapping of the archipelago. As the last gaps were filled in, the existence of more than one Northwest Passage was proven, though the ice blocked attempts to sail all the way through. As one participant, Johann Miertsching, concluded, the now discovered Northwest Passages "are without significance and useless for navigation as long as the climate in these parts is so severe and the sea covered with ice 50 to 60 feet thick."

With the Northwest Passage now mapped, and hence "discovered," there was no further inducement to return to those perilous, ice-choked straits. The Admiralty had, in the course of a few years, lost five ships—*Intrepid*, *Assistance*, *Pioneer*, *Investigator* and *Breadalbane*—in the search

for Franklin. The Americans had lost the brig *Advance*. War with Russia had broken out in the Crimea, claiming Britain's attention. The long search for the Northwest Passage was over; but while the route was known, it was deemed impassable and so no longer of interest. All that remained was Lady Franklin's continued determination to learn her husband's fate.

CHAPTER 7

Franklin's Fate

They forged the last link of the North West Passage with their lives. —SIR JOHN RICHARDSON, 1859

THE SEARCH for Sir John Franklin and his lost expedition was the greatest push into the Arctic ever mounted, involving dozens of ships and thousands of men. Between 1847 and 1859, thirty-two separate expeditions, both by land and by sea, searched the Arctic. At first they sought to rescue the 129 men of *Erebus* and *Terror*, but as the years passed, hope faded, and the task turned to learning the fate of the expedition, the greatest disaster in the annals of Arctic exploration. What had happened? The mystery spurred investigations that have lasted to the present day, to learn how and why a large, well-equipped group, with so much promise and hope, failed. The tragic tale has been slowly wrested from the Arctic through the memories of the Inuit peoples who witnessed the tragedy, and through the study of scattered relics and the bones of the dead by generations of searchers and archaeologists.

A Trail of Bodies and the Last Record

In 1858, Lady Franklin herself dispatched the yacht *Fox*, under the command of Captain Francis Leopold McClintock, to search for her husband. In a letter to McClintock, she noted that after rescuing any possible survivors, "next . . . in importance is the recovery of the unspeakably precious documents of the expedition, public or private, and the personal relics of my dear husband and his companions."

McClintock and *Fox* arrived at Beechey Island in 1858 and then turned south, following Franklin's trail. Arriving at the northern end of the Boothia Peninsula, near Bellot Strait, *Fox* wintered in the ice while McClintock and his officers and men sledged further south. Carl Peterson, a Dane who accompanied them as an interpreter, learned from the Inuit that the ice had sunk two ships near King William Island. Additional relics, including more silverware and uniform buttons, were purchased from the Inuit. On reaching the southern shores of King William Island in early 1859, McClintock spoke to two Inuit who had actually been at the place where the wrecked ships were. After exploring the east coast of King William, McClintock headed north up the island's western shore, where he planned to meet up with Lieutenant George Hobson, in command of another sledging party from *Fox*.

On his way north to meet Hobson, McClintock discovered scattered relics and remains. One skeleton, clad in the tattered remains of a

FACING PAGE Crew on ice clinging to a boat. From *The Arctic World*

THIS PAGE The yacht *Fox*, in which Leopold McClintock sailed to search for Franklin in 1858. From Peterson, *Den Sidste Franklin-Expedition*

steward's blue uniform, lay face down on a gravel ridge close to the beach near Cape Herschel. It was some 135 miles south of where the ships had been abandoned. Near the bones were a handful of possessions, including a hairbrush, notebook and papers belonging to Harry Peglar, *Terror*'s captain of the foretop. One of the papers had words that may have been the dead man's last: "O death whare is thy sting, the grave at Comfort Cove for who has any douat how . . . the dyer sad and whare traffelegar, etc." The skeleton is sometimes identified as Peglar's, though one Franklin historian, R. J. Cyriax, suggested it may be that of Thomas Armitage, gunroom steward aboard *Terror* and a former shipmate of Peglar's prior to their last, fatal voyage together.

Another piece of writing, according to Franklin researcher David Woodman, may indicate preparations made aboard *Terror* just before the ships were abandoned on April 22, 1848.

The "last record" of the Franklin expedition found by Lieutenant George Hobson.
From Peterson, *Den Sidste Franklin-Expedition*

Working with the misspelled, water-stained words, he suggests that the note reads: "We shall have his new boots in middle watch as we have got some very hard ground to heave [we] shall want some grog to wet [our whistles]. All my [heart], Tom for I to[o] do think [it is] time to[go]. . . . the 21st night [agreed]." These few words may be Peglar's, shared with (Tom?) Armitage.

Hobson also made some discoveries. He found two cairns with notes deposited by Franklin's men on the standard Admiralty forms. One cairn, at Back Bay, had a report from Lieutenant Graham Gore. The other cairn, six miles to the north at Victory Point at the north end of King William, had more or less the same report by Lieutenant Graham Gore, with an addendum by Captains Crozier and Fitzjames. Gore's report stated:

> 28 of May 1847. H.M. Ships Erebus and Terror wintered in the ice in Lat. 70°5N, Long. 98°23' W.
>
> Having wintered in 1846–7 at Beechey Island in Lat. 74°43'28" N, Long. 91°39'15" W after having ascended Wellington Channel to Lat. 77° and returned by the west side of Cornwallis Island.
>
> Sir John Franklin commanding the expedition. All well.
>
> Party consisting of two officers and six men left the ships on Monday, 24th May 1847.
>
> Gm. Gore, Lieut.
Charles F. Des Voeux, Mate

Franklin, following instructions, had sailed 150 miles northwest along Devon Island's shores and circumnavigated Cornwallis Island, passing the site of today's settlement of Resolute, before wintering at Beechey Island in 1845–46. The dates in Gore's note were wrong, as shown by the dates on the graves at Beechey. In April 1846, after Braine's death, the ice had cleared enough for *Erebus* and *Terror* to break free and proceed south, probably by way of Peel Sound and Franklin Strait, between Prince of Wales Island and Somerset Island. Caught by the ice, Franklin wintered off the north shore of King William Island and dispatched this party to explore the

Excavating the cairn where the last record was discovered. From *The Arctic World*

surrounding area, as the sun was now returning after months of darkness. They were, at this time, only 90 miles from where Simpson and Dease had ended their expedition, and within sight of lands briefly traversed and named by Ross. If indeed they sledged those 90 miles, Franklin's men closed the gap and found a Northwest Passage. It has been thought, perhaps hopefully, that they did.

In the margins of Gore's report, Captains Crozier and Fitzjames had added notes that told of a year of hardship and imminent disaster:

> 25th April 1848. H.M. Ships Terror and Erebus were deserted on the 22nd April, 5 leagues NNW of this, having been beset since 12th Sept 1846. The officers & crew consisting of 105 souls under the command of Captain F.R.M. Crozier, landed here . . .
>
> Sir John Franklin died on the 11th June, 1847 and the total loss by deaths in the expedition has been to this date 9 officers & 15 men.
>
> F.R.M. Crozier
> Captain & Senior Officer
> and start on tomorrow 26th for Back's Fish River.
>
> James Fitzjames
> Captain H.M.S. Erebus.

After being stuck in the ice for eighteen months, and with a number of deaths, including Franklin's (just two weeks after Gore had been sent out), Crozier had abandoned the ships in the

TOP Dip circle, an instrument for measuring magnetism, abandoned by the Franklin expedition at Victory Point. National Maritime Museum, Greenwich/D4900-7

BOTTOM Snow goggles made by a member of Franklin's crew, found by Leopold McClintock in the abandoned boat at Erebus Bay on King William Island, 1859. National Maritime Museum, Greenwich/ D5228

Medicine Chest from the Franklin Expedition

Measuring just fourteen by thirteen inches, and only five inches deep, this canvas-covered mahogany medicine chest was left at Victory Point by the survivors of the Franklin expedition, presumably on or around April 22, 1848. The chest was discoverd on June 2, 1859, by Lieutenant George Hobson of Leopold McClintock's search expedition. It was found with the lid closed, and apparently had lain undisturbed since being abandoned eleven years earlier.

The chest contains twenty-three bottles of medicines and chemicals and a handful of instruments, such as a pewter syringe. There are also a few metal containers, including one filled with pills. The contents of the bottles were at varying levels, indicating that some had been used by the doctors attached to the Franklin expedition. McClintock, and scholars after him, carefully studied the medicine chest for clues to the fate of the expedition. McClintock believed that scurvy doomed Franklin's men.

Richard J. Cyriax, a physician and Franklin scholar, determined that the remaining medicines indicated treatment for scurvy, as well as for snow blindness, rheumatism, bronchitis and frostbite, all ailments to be expected and indeed found among the crews of Arctic expeditions.

Medicine chest abandoned by the Franklin expedition at Victory Point. National Maritime Museum, Greenwich/A4910

**Discovering one of Franklin's
boats on King William Island,
1858–59.** From *The Arctic World*

ice and headed for land. Around the cairn where the last record was found, Hobson and McClintock reported that a large quantity of stores had been landed and piled in heaps, including stoves, clothing and equipment. There was a sextant marked with the name of Frederick John Hornby (one of the mates on *Terror*); a circular brass plate, probably broken out of a wooden gun case, engraved with the name of Charles H. Osmer (paymaster and purser on *Erebus*), and wooden canteens marked with the names of William Hedges and William Heather (two of the Royal Marines on *Terror*).

To the searchers, it appeared that the pile was made up of unnecessary articles. "Around the cairn," wrote McClintock, "a vast quantity of clothing and stores lay strewed about, as if at this spot every article was thrown away which could possibly be dispensed with—such as pickaxes, shovels, boats, cooking stoves, ironwork, rope, blocks, canvas, oars and medicine chest." To later historians, however, the assemblage on the beach appeared to be a cache of supplies to be returned to, stored in safer circumstances than aboard ships that the ice might sink. `

Crozier, Fitzjames and their men had marched south, along King William's western shores, toward the Adelaide Peninsula and the mouth of the Great Fish River. And there, along the way, they had fallen, individually or in groups. The Inuit tales recounted to Dr. John Rae now made sense, with a final party falling within a day or two's march from the river's mouth.

As McClintock and Hobson travelled north together, back to *Fox*, they found a ship's boat resting on a solidly built oak sledge. Lines running from the sledge indicated that the crew had pulled it, the boat on it and the stores piled inside (which McClintock estimated weighed some 1,400 lbs.!) across the ice and snow. The abandoned boat's bow pointed northeast, suggesting to McClintock that this was a party returning to the ships. The boat held a range of stores and the skeletons of two men. One was in

the bow, much disturbed by animals. The other "was in a somewhat more perfect state, and was enveloped with clothes and furs; it lay across the boat, under the after-thwart. Close beside it were found five watches; and there were two double-barrelled guns—one barrel in each loaded and cocked—standing muzzle upwards against the boat's side." Twenty-six pieces of silverware were also found, eight of them marked with Franklin's crest, the others with "the crests or initials of nine different officers." One of the pocket watches found in the boat had belonged to Edward Couch, a mate aboard *Erebus*.

McClintock and Hobson's discoveries confirmed Rae's reports that the expedition had met with disaster and augmented the older Inuit accounts with new ones about men who "dropped by the way." McClintock noted that the last record found in the cairn was a perfect model of "official brevity. No log-book could be more laconic." But it did offer a few more facts and clues about where the ships had gone and what had happened.

Later Traces

Lady Franklin's determination and eloquence, particularly in one letter she wrote in April 1856 to spur the British government to continue the search, was touching:

> What secrets may be hidden within those wrecked or stranded ships we know not—what may be buried in the graves of our unhappy countrymen or in caches not yet discovered we have yet to learn. The bodies and the graves we were told of have not yet been found; the books (journals) . . . have not been recovered, and thus left in ignorance and darkness with so little obtained and so much yet to learn, can it be said and is it fitting to pronounce that the fate of the expedition is ascertained?

As researcher David Woodman points out, these poignant words "have led many in the intervening century and a half to take up the tale of the Franklin tragedy anew."

The shores of King William Island today. John Harrington

Not content to leave the story of the lost Franklin expedition at the point where McClintock had left off, an American explorer, Charles Francis Hall, decided to continue the search. Some of Franklin's men, he thought, might have settled with the Inuit. Between 1860 and 1869 he made extensive trips to the north to live among the Inuit and seek more traces. They told him about a series of graves on the western shore of King William Island, close to James Ross Point. There, digging into the snow, Hall uncovered a complete skeleton that he sent to the United States. In 1872, the skeleton was sent to England, where it was identified as that of Lieutenant Henry Le Vesconte of the *Erebus*. Lady Franklin's companion and secretary, Sophia Cracroft, in a February 1873 letter, wrote:

> The remains were examined & described by Professor Huxley, & the result has been all but certain identification with Mr. Le Vesconte, on account of the height, the very prominent nose, & massive lower jaw, which were all remarkable characteristics of Mr. Le Vesconte. The peculiarities too of the teeth (one of which was stopped in gold) are also identified by his family, who have, I believe, no doubt on the question.

The remains were buried in a vault near the Painted Hall at the Royal Naval College at Greenwich and marked with a marble bas-relief plaque.

The Inuit also told Hall about a body on a nearby point that David Woodman believes is modern Booth Point. According to the Inuit, the body, which they dug up and left exposed, "presented a terrible sight about his lower gums."

In June and July 1981, forensic anthropologist Owen Beattie retraced Hall's route and at the same site discovered a partial skeleton, portions of the skull and bones from the legs and arms. With them, Beattie and archaeologist James M. Savelle found a shell button and a fragment of a clay pipe. Beattie's examination showed that the deceased was a Caucasian male, about

twenty-five years old. The bones showed definite traces of scurvy and marks that may have come from a saw. While noting that the intervening years of exposure and gnawing by animals made definitive conclusions very difficult, Beattie thought the possible saw cuts and the fact that the central portion of the body was missing suggested parts of it may have been eaten by starving survivors. He also found an elevated lead count that was ten times higher than samples of Inuit skeletal material gathered nearby. This indicated that lead poisoning may have played a role in the Franklin disaster—a theme to which Beattie would return with remains found at other Franklin sites.

Inspired by Hall's accounts, another American, Lieutenant Frederick Schwatka of the United States Army, spent the better part of 1879 searching King William Island and the Adelaide Peninsula for traces of the Franklin expedition. He made a number of discoveries, including another complete skeleton at Victory Point. McClintock and Hobson had missed it, but Inuit accounts told of finding a dead man near a large pile of clothes there. A fragment of a telescope, gilt buttons from an officer's uniform and a medal, marked "Second Mathematical Prize, Royal Naval College, Awarded to John Irving, Midsummer 1830," seemed to show this was the grave of Lieutenant Irving, late of HMS *Terror*. Schwatka thought that the body had been buried by a group of men who had returned to the site. This was one of the first clues that the simple tale suggested by the last record might not be accurate and that not all of the expedition had slowly marched south, dying along the way.

Schwatka also found the boat that McClintock had discovered and buried the remains of four men lying nearby. He sent the stem of the boat to England, where today it is in the collections of the National Maritime Museum, Greenwich.

Investigating Inuit tales, Schwatka found evidence that some members of the expedition had left King William Island and reached the mainland.

Charles Francis Hall and his Inuit interpreters, Tookoolito and Ebierbing. From Hall, *Arctic Researches*

On the Adelaide Peninsula, he was led to a spot where some Inuit claimed that the remains of a ship's boat and a number of skeletons lay. Deep snow covered the site, which Schwatka named Starvation Cove. Through the years, other searchers, some Inuit and others guided by Inuit tales, have returned to the peninsula to look for more clues at what they believe to be the end of the line for the Franklin expedition.

In the 1920s, more relics and human skeletons were discovered. Anthropologist Knud Rasmussen, in 1923, found "a number of human bones . . . some pieces of cloth and stumps of leather. . . ." at Richardson Point, east of Starvation Cove. Three years later, trader Peter Norberg found the skull of a Franklin crew member on the northern shore of the Adelaide Peninsula near modern Thunder Bay.

Frederick Schwatka, surrounded by interested Inuit, shows them a copy of *The Illustrated London News* during his search for Franklin records and relics 1879.
From *The Illustrated London News*, 1 January 1881

Macabre Relics, Traces of the Dead

Hundreds of relics were brought back from the Arctic by the various expeditions searching for Sir John Franklin, and by later explorers looking for clues to the expedition's demise. Silver forks and spoons belonging to the officers, a simple knife marked with the name of caulker's mate Cornelius Hickey, medals, a collar with the name of Lieutenant Frederick Des Voeux inked into it, and many other personal effects are grim reminders of the fate of their owners. The debris of a lost expedition, the sundry objects were scattered across the length of King William Island and the surrounding area, found by Inuit who later traded them to Franklin searchers. For a researcher going through drawers of relics in museum collections in England, Canada and the United States, the emotional impact is like that of sorting through personal effects in the morgue.

The skull of one of Franklin's men, found on King William Island. John Harrington

In the 1930s, Hudson's Bay Company trader H. A. Learmonth reported that an elderly Inuit woman, Neniook, told him that as a child she had seen the "skeletons of seven men still partly clothed in blue serge, and partly buried in the sand and seaweed on a small island in the vicinity" of Starvation Cove. In 1936, Learmonth and his assistant D. G. Sturrock discovered the bones of three men, an ivory button and a silver English half-crown dated 1820 some 15 miles west of Starvation Cove.

A series of discoveries was made by Hudson's Bay Company trader William Gibson in the 1930s. At the south end of King William Island, near the site of today's Gjoa Haven, he found a number of skeletons. On one of the offshore Todd Islets, Gibson also found the remains of four skeletons buried in the sand of a low spit. "These skeletons," he wrote, "had been well preserved in the moist sand and patches of the blue naval broadcloth held together and were taken away by us." On another island, Gibson found the remains of seven men. He collected the skulls and scattered bones, then buried them beneath a large stone cairn.

These discoveries have led researcher David Woodman to question whether Starvation Cove was indeed the end of the line. He has carefully examined Inuit accounts gathered by Hall and Schwatka, as well as the physical evidence. Woodman feels that the various sites, when matched to Inuit tales of the end of the Franklin expedition, point to a different interpretation than the one suggested by the last record. That record, he argues, suggests what the expedition *intended* to do, while the scattered remains show what *some of them* did.

Woodman's reconstruction of what happened, drawing strongly on Inuit testimony, has Crozier leading the bulk of his party south to the Great Fish River in 1848 to hunt and fish before returning to the ships. The area around the river's mouth was well known from the accounts of earlier explorers as being rich in game. The

ships, abandoned because of scurvy, could be remanned by crews restored to health by fresh provisions. This would corroborate Inuit accounts of going aboard *Erebus* and *Terror* and meeting officers and sailors after 1848.

Sometime later, perhaps after the winter of 1849–50, the ships may have been abandoned again. Inuit accounts mention that one ship was thrown on its side and wrecked near shore, while another ship, fast in the ice, drifted south. It would be at this time that the last group of men set out for the south. Woodman suggests that the forty men encountered by the Inuit and described to Rae was this group. They were seen by the Inuit, not in 1848 as argued by later historians, but in 1851. Inuit stories emphasize that a smaller group of men, weakened and starving, wintered with them. Some of the kablunat died, but a last, small group left, walking south for home, in 1852. They never made it.

Inuit Testimony

Modern researchers like David C. Woodman and Dorothy Harley Eber are increasingly turning to the oral traditions and testimony of the Inuit to learn more about the fate of the Franklin expedition. A few early searchers, notably John Rae of the Hudson's Bay Company and Charles Francis Hall, did rely on Inuit informants, but for the most part Europeans of the day and a number of later historians discounted them. However, with no survivors, minimal records, and only a trail of abandoned gear, personal effects and scattered bones, the sole substantial body of evidence is Inuit testimony. Moreover, the drama of the disastrous end of the Franklin expedition was played out in front of Inuit witnesses on lands they knew well. Working with Inuit testimony collected by Hall in the 1860s, Woodman has followed the trail of Franklin's last men and offers convincing evidence that some survived until at least 1851 and that a handful almost made it out of the Arctic.

On Beechey Island, the markers of the graves of John Torrington and John **Hartnell, the first members of the Franklin expedition to die.** Owen Beattie

That the Franklin expedition was afflicted with scurvy is certain, both from Inuit accounts and from the forensic work undertaken by Owen Beattie and James Savelle. In July 1982, they rediscovered the fragmentary remains of the boat found by McClintock and Hobson in 1859, and then by Schwatka in 1879. Beattie's team also found the complete sole of a boot with three large screws driven through it to create "makeshift cleats that would have given the wearer a grip on ice and snow." Skeletal remains of several individuals were discovered, "scattered along the coast for a kilometre to the north" of the boat. This suggested to Beattie and Savelle that "those pulling the lifeboat could go no further, abandoned the lifeboat and themselves died a short time later as they walked toward the ships."

In all, Beattie felt, the scattered skeletal remains, could have come from as many as fourteen or as few as six men. The bones showed the scarring and pitting caused by scurvy, and analysis showed high levels of lead, suggesting again that Franklin's men had suffered from lead poisoning. Lead poisoning can lead to a number of side effects, such as anorexia, weakness and fatigue, paranoia, irritability and anaemia. Could these have affected the judgement of the officers and men and contributed to the disaster? To test his theory, Beattie proposed excavating the three graves at Beechey Island, where the frozen ground would have preserved the bodies of the first three men to die during the Franklin expedition.

In 1984, and again in 1986, Beattie flew to Beechey Island to exhume the bodies. Parks Canada archaeologists had surveyed the island between 1976 and 1981, noting that after more than a century of visits, little except for a few scraps of wood, tin and the rock outlines of structures had survived from Franklin's winter camp. But the graves held more promise. Digging through the hard-packed permafrost, Beattie and his crew uncovered the wooden coffins of the three men. Two of the coffins had hand-painted metal plaques, with the names, ages

"Frozen in time," twenty-year-old John Torrington, the first man to die on Franklin's expedition, as he appeared when unearthed by scientists seeking to learn if lead poisoning had played a part in the disaster. Owen Beattie

Scoured by Arctic winds and weathered by the years, John Torrington's grave marker.
Owen Beattie

"Preserved" Food

A relatively new feature aboard *Erebus* and *Terror* were the "preserved" foods, packed in "tins." In the early nineteenth century, the advent of canned food (the process was patented in England in 1811) had gradually introduced their use to some ships, and other Arctic expeditions had also carried "preserved" food. Franklin's expedition was supplied with tinned meat, vegetables and soup by London merchant Stephan Goldner. The 8,000 cans he provided were large, stamped with the words "Goldner Patent" and painted red.

The "preserved" meats were boiled and roast beef, boiled and roast mutton, seasoned beef, beef and vegetables, soup with stewed meat, ox-cheek, and veal. The "preserved" vegetables were potatoes, carrots, parsnips, and combinations of the three.

The "preserved" meat gained much notoriety when Franklin searchers reported that a large cairn of several hundred empty meat tins had been left behind by the expedition when it sailed from Beechey Island. The quantity of meat seemed, to the searchers, too large to have been eaten in the course of the year the ships wintered at Beechey. It was suggested that the meat was bad and had been discarded. Sir John Richardson in particular blamed the loss of the expedition on bad meat, basing his conclusions in part on the fact that canned meat provided by Goldner to the Royal Navy after Franklin had sailed was found unfit to eat and condemned (rejected).

In more recent times, the tins once again became the focus of inquiry after researcher Owen Beattie performed autopsies on the bodies of three of Franklin's men and found evidence of lead poisoning, apparently from the lead solder used to seal the tins.

A tin can of food, probably soup, from the Franklin expedition, discovered in an Inuit cache near Cape Maria Louisa by Lieutenant Frederick Schwatka, 1878–1879. National Maritime Museum, Greenwich

Cache of tinned or "preserved" food on Beechey Island. Roger Amy and Owen Beattie

and dates of death. Thawing the ice that filled each coffin with hot water, the researchers exposed the clothed bodies, which they stripped, examined, autopsied and X-rayed, then carefully reburied.

They discovered that Hartnell, the second man to die, had been exhumed and autopsied in 1852 by one of the search expeditions. But the most significant discovery, wrested from the bone, hair and tissue samples, was that all three men had high levels of lead. The lead poisoning itself had not killed them. Torrington had died of pneumonia, with complications from an earlier history of tuberculosis. However, in Beattie's opinion, lead poisoning had hastened the young sailor's death, as well as those of his two grave mates. Beattie theorized that lead poisoning had affected the entire expedition, sapping their strength and clouding their judgement, as well as combining with the effects of scurvy, starvation and the extreme cold to inexorably bring about their deaths.

In recent years, other researchers have continued to scour the landscape for further traces. In 1992, 1993 and 1994, photographer and Franklin scholar Barry Ranford surveyed King William Island's shores and found additional relics, including a boat and human bones.

Archaeologist Margaret Bertulli and physical anthropologist Anne Keenleyside, studying the boat site in 1993 and 1994, unearthed the remains of at least eight individuals, as well as a number of small, scattered artifacts: the sole of a boot, rivets from the boat's fastenings, buttons, shreds of fabric, even a broken comb. Keenleyside found definite evidence of cut marks on the finger and rib bones—sure signs of cannibalism—and elevated levels of lead, supporting Beattie's conclusions.

At the same time that Ranford was surveying King William Island, others were searching the waters off its coast, and further south, for the wrecks of *Erebus* and *Terror*. Inuit accounts describe two ships sinking, one close to shore, the other in deeper water—and fragments of a ship or ships have been found in the islands south of King William in Queen Maud Gulf. Tantalizing traces—a Caucasian skull, a piece of ship's copper and the bottom of a mid-nineteenth century British coffee pot—were discovered in 1997 near Kirkwall Island, where David Woodman believes one of the ships, probably *Terror*, now lies. But the wrecks themselves, the grave of Franklin (presumably buried by his crew), and more cached records from the lost expedition remain elusive. Until some or all of these are discovered—if ever—it is unlikely that more of the story will be revealed.

For now, as Barry Ranford noted: "The clues are a detective's nightmare, a heady mixture of fact, fiction and legend Even though the Inuit accounts are proving to be far more accurate than earlier chroniclers believed or acknowledged, the story is often like the weather of King William Island: shrouded in a foggy mist, with important details missing or blurred."

But the allure of that fog-shrouded coast and the dream of sailing a ship all the way through the Northwest Passage remained strong.

Monument to Sir John Franklin at Westminster Abbey, London, bearing the epitaph by Tennyson.
The Dean and Chapter of Westminster/Box 11 (1)

The Northwest Passage Conquered

I, too, would suffer in a cause—not in the blazing desert on the way to Jerusalem, but in the frozen North on the way to new knowledge in the unpierced unknown.
—ROALD ENGEBRETH GRAVNING AMUNDSEN, 1928

INSPIRED BY TALES of the lost Franklin expedition and of the many searchers who sought him, a new generation of explorers returned to the Arctic in the early twentieth century. Their goal was to conquer the deadly waterway and to sail from one coast to the other through the ice-clogged straits.

Beginning with the 1902 expedition of Norwegian Otto Sverdrup, the northern islands of the Arctic archipelago—including Banks, Ellesmere, Axel Heiberg, Amund Ringnes, Ellef Ringnes, Borden, Brock, Bathurst Longheed and Melville—were completely or partially circumnavigated by ship and sledge, and mapped. But it was the Norwegian explorer Roald Amundsen whose determination finally guided a ship all the way through the Northwest Passage. Amundsen, in the small sloop *Gjøa*, sailed through the Northwest Passage on his first attempt, becoming the first to traverse the long-sought and heavily paid-for sea route.

The thirty-one-year-old Amundsen had trained for years to become an explorer. Bathing in the icy waters of fjords, skiing and playing football to toughen himself, he was spurred on by reading about Franklin's struggles, privations and death. But Amundsen was as astute as he was driven. He gained the confidence of Norwegian polar explorer Fridtjof Nansen, whose *Fram* expedition of 1893–96 had drifted across the Arctic Ocean, held fast in the ice for three years. Nansen supported Amundsen's ambitions and offered helpful advice.

From his research, Amundsen learned that conflict had often arisen between Arctic explorers and the navigators or masters of the ships that carried them north. To avoid that, he decided to go to sea to obtain his own master's certificate. Working aboard a Norwegian polar sealer, he

rose to the rank of mate. As mate, he joined Adrien de Gerlache de Gomery's 1897–99 *Belgica* expedition to Antarctica, gaining invaluable experience.

Amundsen's plans for an Arctic expedition centred on a bold dream that would make him world famous—the conquest of the Northwest Passage. From the pinnacle of this success, he could push for his ultimate goal—to be the first to reach both the North and South Poles. But he also needed "a scientific purpose as well as the purpose of exploration. Otherwise, I should not be taken seriously and would not get backing." So Amundsen pursued "studies in magnetic science and . . . the methods of taking magnetic observations." He planned to re-establish the location of the north magnetic pole, plotted for the first time by James Clark Ross on King William Island in 1831.

The next step was to acquire a vessel, and Amundsen chose the 72-foot-long *Gjøa*, then working out of Norway's Arctic port of Tromsø. He wrote: "She was a small fishing smack from the northern part of Norway. She was fortyseven tons and of the same age as myself." The tiny *Gjøa* was a perfect choice for manoeuvring through the shallow and ice-choked straits of the Northwest Passage. Amundsen added a 13-horsepower diesel engine that drove a small iron propeller. The engine "was the pet of everyone on board," wrote Amundsen. "Our successful negotiation of the North West Passage was very largely due to our excellent little engine." That, and Amundsen's astute realization that "what has not been accomplished with large vessels and main force I will attempt with a small vessel and patience."

In the spring of 1903, Amundsen readied for the voyage, raising funds, gathering supplies and loading *Gjøa* with tons of stores and provisions. "The large, peculiarly built provision boxes were stowed and closely packed like children's bricks in a box. So neatly was this done that we found space on our little *Gjøa* for food and

FACING PAGE Roald Amundsen, posing in his furs in a Kristiana (Oslo) studio, **1899.** Universitetsbiblioteket, Oslo

equipment, enough and to spare *for five years.*" The provisions included food for sled dogs—Amundsen was determined to not follow the British tradition of man-hauled sledges. He included dogs of both sexes to ensure a steady supply during the voyage.

Amundsen also assembled a six-man crew: Godfred Hansen (a former Danish naval officer), second-in-command, navigator, astronomer, geologist and photographer; Anton Lund (a Tromsø-born Arctic whaler), first mate; Peder Ristvedt, Norwegian-born first engineer and meteorologist; Helmer Hansen, a Norwegian Arctic veteran; Gustav Juel Wiik, a Norwegian trained at the Magnetic Observatory in Potsdam, second engineer and Amundsen's assistant for magnetic observations; and Adolf Henrik Lindstrom (a Norwegian veteran of Nansen's second *Fram* expedition), the cook.

Gjøa slipped out of Kristiana (now Oslo) harbour on the night of June 16, 1903, in a heavy rain squall. That morning, Amundsen had been confronted by an angry creditor who demanded payment within twenty-four hours, or he would

Gjøa

The 46.6-ton *Gjøa*, the conqueror of the Northwest Passage, is only 69 feet long. But she is broad, with a 20-foot, 6-inch beam and a 9-foot depth of hold. Normally, *Gjøa* drew 7 feet, 7 inches, but Roald Amundsen loaded her so heavily for his attempt on the Northwest Passage that she drew 10 feet. Sloop rigged, with one mast, *Gjøa* carried a mainsail, forestaysail, jib, flying jib and a gaff topsail—313 square yards of canvas that pushed her to up to 10 knots in a stiff breeze.

Gjøa was built in 1872 at the Rosendal shipyard of Knut Johannesson Skaale in Norway. The first owner, Asbjørn Sexe, named her after his wife, Gjøa, and used the ship to fish herring. After being wrecked in 1882, *Gjøa* was rebuilt as a sealer and sold to H. C. Johannesen of Tromsø. She worked the "polar seas," in Amundsen's words, for the next eighteen years, so was an ideal choice for his expedition when he bought her in 1901.

After a summer voyage in the Polar Sea in 1901, Amundsen sailed south to Trondjhem, where *Gjøa* was hauled out at the engineering works of Isidor Nielsen. There the hull was strengthened, the frames and floors were doubled, and a three-inch-thick oak sheathing was added to the bow. The stem was reinforced with iron straps to resist the ice, and the hold was reinforced with ice beams and stanchions.

Amundsen also installed an engine—a small, two-cylinder 13-horsepower "Dan" type kerosene-burner—along with "petroleum tanks built to the shape of the boat." The hold and crew's quarters are small, so Amundsen had to carefully pack every space. The crew quarters measure only 6 by 9 feet, not much room for eight men to live in for three years in the Arctic.

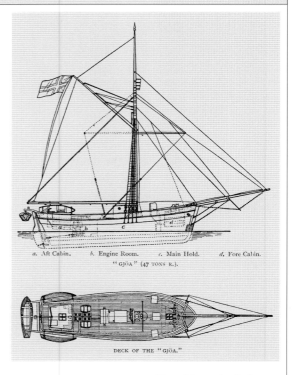

a. Aft Cabin. b. Engine Room. c. Main Hold. d. Fore Cabin.
"GJÖA" (47 TONS R.).

DECK OF THE "GJÖA."

Plan of Amundsen's sloop
Gjøa. From Amundsen, *The North West Passage*

have the vessel seized and have Amundsen arrested for fraud. "The ruin of my years of work seemed imminent," wrote Amundsen, and so "I resolved upon a desperate expedient."

After stopping at Godhaven to pick up twenty sled dogs, Amundsen proceeded to Dalyrmple Rock to load provisions and gasoline. *Gjøa* then headed west, on Franklin's track, along Melville Strait into the Arctic archipelago. When *Gjøa* arrived at Beechey on August 22, 1903, Amundsen wrote: "The heaviness and sadness of death hang over Beechey Island." The crew of *Gjøa* "found the whole completely ruined." But for Amundsen, the place was magic. "I was on holy ground," he enthused, and, in his mind's eye, he imagined *Erebus* and *Terror* at anchor, with Franklin coming ashore and decide that this would be where they wintered.

Captivated like other observers before and since by the scene of Franklin's tragedy, Amundsen wrote: "The dark outlines of crosses marking graves inland are silent witnesses before my eyes as I sit here. . . . it is the farewell of the Franklin expedition. From this point it passed into darkness—and death." Departing Beechey, Amundsen paid tribute to Franklin and his men: "Let us raise a monument to them, more enduring than stone; the recognition that they were the first discoverers of the Passage."

Moving south, still in the wake of *Erebus* and *Terror*, *Gjøa* entered Peel Strait. Pushing farther south and into the ice, Amundsen noted: "Our voyage now assumed a new character. Hitherto we had been sailing in safe and known waters. Now we were making our way through waters never sailed in . . . and were hoping to reach still farther where no keel had ever ploughed." On entering Franklin Strait, the proximity of the north magnetic pole affected the compass. "The needle of the compass, which had gradually been losing its capacity for self-adjustment, now absolutely declined to act. We were thus reduced to steering by the stars, like our forefathers the Vikings."

***Gjøa* and her crew members, 1903.** Universitetsbiblioteket, Oslo

Sailing on, *Gjøa* reached the De la Roquette Islands. The last ship to even come near them was *Pandora*, on Allen Young's private attempt to navigate the Northwest Passage in 1875, and she had been blocked by an impenetrable wall of ice. Amundsen fretted that the ice would be there—a barrier to thwart him in his conquest of the passage. But as *Gjøa* sailed on, the ship began to slowly lurch. "It was a swell under the boat, a swell—a message from the open sea. The water to the south was open. . . . I cast my eyes over our little *Gjøa* from stem to stern, from the deck to the mast top, and smiled."

But the voyage was far from over, and disaster loomed. In Sir James Ross Strait, *Gjøa* ran aground hard, but after working the engine and sails, managed to get free. That evening, the vessel was nearly lost when a fire broke out in the engine room, "right among the tanks holding 2,200 gallons of petroleum." Quick action and a bucket brigade extinguished the flames and saved the ship.

Three days later, *Gjøa* ran aground again, this time on a large submerged reef off Matty Island. The ship hit at high tide and drew too much water to get away. The men threw twenty-five of the heaviest cases of provisions overboard, but still could not get *Gjøa* free. The next day, a storm blew in, and Amundsen decided "as a last resource, to try and get her off with the sails." With all canvas set, "the mighty press of sail and the high choppy sea, combined, had the effect of lifting the vessel up, and pitching her forward again among the rocks, so that we expected every moment to see her planks scattered on the sea. The false keel was splintered, and floated up.

Amundsen and his crew celebrating Christmas aboard *Gjøa*, 1903. From Amundsen, *The North west Passage*

All we could do was to watch the course of events and calmly await the issue."

As *Gjøa* approached the reef, now bare and exposed, Amundsen and the crew threw more of their heavy deckload of cases of provisions overboard. "The spray and sleet were washing over the vessel, the mast trembled, and the *Gjøa* seemed to pull herself together for a last final leap. She was lifted up high and flung bodily on to the bare rocks, bump, bump—with terrific force. . . . Yet another thump, worse than ever, then one more, and we slid off."

Moving on farther south through Rae Strait, *Gjøa* worked her way through groups of small

islands, between the mainland and King William Island. Approaching the southern end of the island on September 9, Amundsen anchored in a "small harbour quite sheltered from the wind, a veritable haven of rest for us weary travellers," which they named Gjøahavn. From their vantage point, they saw that Simpson Strait, lying to the west, was clear of ice. "The Northwest Passage was therefore open to us. But our first and foremost task was to obtain exact data as to the Magnetic North Pole, and so the Passage, being of less importance, had to be left in abeyance."

Anchoring close to the beach, Amundsen and his crew unloaded their supplies and built a series

Netsilik visitors to *Gjøa* at Gjøahavn.
Universitetsbiblioteket, Oslo

of huts and observatories on the shore, using their wooden packing crates to form the walls of the buildings. During the eighteen-month stay, Amundsen and Wiik used a series of sophisticated devices—fourteen magnets, three inclinatoria for determining inclination and two instruments to measure declination—to record fluctuations in the earth's magnetism. Amundsen's land expeditions in 1904 and 1905 measured magnetism on King William Island, helping him to pinpoint the north magnetic pole. He found that it had migrated some 40 miles northeast from where Ross had first located it in June 1831.

Amundsen and his crew were not at Gjøahavn long before groups of Netsilik Inuit began to visit their camp. "This was a truly thrilling moment" noted Amundsen. "No one of them had ever seen a white man before, yet white men were a part of the legendary tradition of their tribe. Seventy-two years earlier, their grandfathers had met Sir James Clark Ross on almost this very ground." Amundsen welcomed the Inuit and traded iron for skin clothing and food. In time, some two hundred Inuit men, women and children were encamped among the Norwegians.

Amundsen carefully studied his neighbours, collecting a large quantity of tools, weapons,

Gjøa arrives in Nome,
Alaska, in August 1906, after
successfully navigating the
Northwest Passage. Vancouver
Maritime Museum/no number

clothing and other implements of everyday life. His interest was more than that of an amateur anthropologist or ethnographer—he wanted to learn from the Inuit how to live off the land and survive. To preserve harmony, Amundsen asked his men to refrain from intercourse with the Inuit women. Always one to hedge his bets, though, in a show of "white man's magic," Amundsen invited the Inuit aboard *Gjøa* and then blew up an old abandoned igloo, seemingly by only waving his hand, to dissuade any thoughts of attack on the small Norwegian contingent.

After dismantling their camp, the expedition sailed from Gjøahavn on August 13, 1905. Proceeding slowly, with a lookout in the crowsnest and with the lead line constantly employed in the uncharted waters, they passed the southwest tip of King William Island as the fog lifted.

As *Gjøa* proceeded west, her shallow draft again saved the day as Amundsen threaded the ship through shallows and rocks on all sides. "The lead," he wrote, "flew up and down, down and up, and the man at the helm had to pay close attention and keep his eye on the look-out man who jumped in the crow's nest like a maniac, throwing his arms about for starboard and port." Entering Victoria Strait, Amundsen sailed into Cambridge Bay, anchoring on the morning of August 17. *Gjøa* was now back in waters where other ships had sailed, having completed the last "unsolved link in the North West Passage."

Nine days later, continuing west, *Gjøa* encountered the whaler *Charles Hansson*, out of San Francisco. It was "magical," Amundsen later recalled, "I could feel tears coming to my eyes." Ice halted *Gjøa*'s progress at King Point, on the Yukon coast. Close by the wreck of the American whaler *Bonanza*, driven ashore in a sinking condition by her crew, Amundsen anchored to spend a third winter in the Arctic.

Impatient to telegraph news of his triumphant passage to the newspapers that had agreed to pay for exclusive rights to his story, Amundsen set off by dogsled for Eagle City, Alaska, some 500 miles

***Gjøa* preserved ashore at the Norsk Sjøfartsmuseum, Oslo.**
James P. Delgado

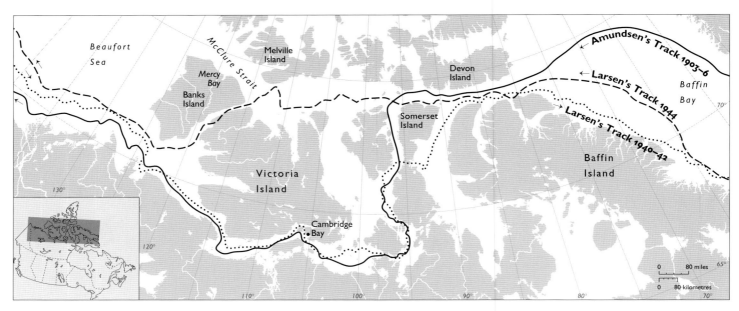

distant. There, at Fort Egbert, was the end of the United States Army's telegraph line into Alaska. Amundsen cabled a thousand-word report. The news of his triumph was picked up by American newspapers, doubtless leaked from the telegraph stations on the way, and the papers that had secured exclusive rights, particularly *The Times*, in London, refused to pay. This financial blow, however, paled in the face of the loss of two *Gjøa* crew members. Gustav Wiik took ill in March 1906, and despite Amundsen's best efforts at doctoring, died. He was buried ashore at King Point. The other death was that of a young Inuk named Manni, who had joined the crew at King William Island. While hunting in an open boat, Manni stood up to fire his shotgun, and the recoil knocked him into the water. He never surfaced.

Gjøa departed King Point on July 10, 1906, working through the ice, and after a brief stop at Herschel Island, pushed along the Alaskan coast. On August 30, *Gjøa* sailed through the Bering Strait into the North Pacific. Amundsen brought up a bottle of whiskey, and he and the crew toasted their success with a brief "skoal." *Gjøa* and her crew were feted in Nome, and then, at voyage's end, in San Francisco, where, on a bright October day, Amundsen left the ship as a gift to

the people and city. "Having achieved the first ambition of my life," he "began looking about for new worlds to conquer." They would be the South Pole, by sled, in 1911; the Northeast Passage, in his newly built ship *Maud*, between 1918 and 1923, and the North Pole, by airship, in 1926. These later achievements, would, in time, eclipse his first. But it was thirty-six years before another ship, this time in a demonstration of Canadian sovereignty, traversed the Northwest Passage.

Asserting Canadian Sovereignty

Britain, its interest in the Northwest Passage at an end, had ceded its interest in the Arctic to the new Dominion of Canada in 1880, largely to forestall American claims to the archipelago. Yet Canada had done little to claim, hold or protect its interests in the Arctic, leaving it to whalers, traders, occasional explorers and missionaries. Many of these were foreigners, including Norwegians and Danes who contested Canada's ownership and control of the Arctic archipelago.

Ottawa had remained unworried about the north until the influx of American gold seekers into the Yukon induced it to send in the North West Mounted Police in 1894. A few years later, the Canadian government began to view the major American whaling outpost on Herschel Island, 90 miles past the United States-Canadian border, as a threat to its claims of sovereignty in the Arctic. Missionary complaints that the whalers who wintered at Herschel were "debauching" the Inuit were another concern. Plans to send the Mounted Police into the Arctic to establish a detachment at Herschel Island had been tentatively formulated in 1900, but it was not until 1903 that the Mounties made their first patrol of the island and the surrounding region.

Despite the difficulties of supply and isolation, and the hardships of a barren, desolate land, the Mounties established a permanent post on Herschel Island. The two-man detachment collected customs, maintained law and order, and stopped the trading of liquor to the Inuit. Over the next few years, the force, now renamed the Royal Northwest Mounted Police, established other posts on Hudson Bay and in the eastern Arctic. Canada's interest in the north was growing, particularly after Otto Sverdrup's 1902 northern islands expedition and Amundsen's traverse of the Northwest Passage in 1903–6.

In 1904, as part of a national plan by the government of Sir Wilfrid Laurier to assert sovereignty in the Arctic, the Canadian Polar Expedition, under the command of Joseph Elzear Bernier, was diverted from its intended three-year exploration of the maritime approaches to the North Pole. Instead, Bernier and his vessel, *Arctic*, were placed under the command of Mounted Police Superintendent J. D. Moodie and sent north to "show the flag," as well as to serve as a base for patrols through the region. In a series of three voyages (1906–7, 1908–9 and 1910–11), the "eastern Arctic Patrol" of the Mounted Police and Captain Bernier left a series of plaques and cairns proclaiming Canada's ownership of the Arctic archipelago. During the 1908–9 expedition, ice conditions were such, in Bernier's opinion, that "if our instructions had included the making of the North West Passage, I feel confident that it could have been made."

Bernier and *Arctic*

The voyages of Quebec-born Joseph Elzear Bernier after the turn of the century strengthened Canada's claim to the Arctic archipelago. Born in 1852, Bernier grew up fascinated with tales of the north, and dreamed of one day conquering the North Pole. While he never achieved the pole, Bernier did navigate the waters of the Northwest Passage, building depots and monuments to mark Canada's possession, and planting the flag to assert the nation's sovereignty. It was an important task, for Canada's claims were being disputed by a number of nations, including Norway and the United States.

In 1904, the Canadian government purchased the German polar exploration ship *Gauss*, renamed it *Arctic*, and sent it to northern Hudson Bay under Bernier's command. During this first voyage, two Inuit visited *Arctic*, bearing letters from Roald Amundsen, then wintering at Gjøahavn and about to complete his transit of the Northwest Passage.

Bernier and *Arctic* returned to the North in 1906–7, cruising up Baffin Bay and through Lancaster Sound, reaching Melville Island before turning back. A stop at Beechey Island gave Bernier and his crew an opportunity to repair the monument left there by the British in memory of Franklin and others who had lost their lives on the quest for the Northwest Passage. They also hauled

John Ross's yacht *Mary* back up onto the beach from where the ice had dragged her. After wintering near Pond Inlet, they pushed down Prince Regent Inlet, but were stopped by ice from going through Fury and Hecla Strait.

Arctic returned in 1908–9, this time in an attempt to reach Banks Island, and, if possible, to sail through the Northwest Passage. But ice, which had stopped Parry in 1819, also blocked Bernier, and he and his crew moored at Winter Harbour. Like the British before him, he mounted a series of long-ranging sled journeys throughout the winter. In August 1909, *Arctic* broke out of Winter Harbour and again tried the passage, but was caught in the ice and pushed back.

In 1910–11, Bernier attempted the Northwest Passage through McClure Strait. Thwarted by the ice,

he wintered at Arctic Bay on Admiralty Inlet. After ice blocked a return home through Fury and Hecla Strait, he pushed north, out of Lancaster Sound and out of Baffin Bay.

Bernier returned to the Arctic on private expeditions between 1912 and 1927, and died in December 1934. The great Canadian explorer is remembered to this day for his voyages underscoring Canada's claims to the north, for retracing the tracks of the great British explorers who had sought the Northwest Passage, for repairing and constructing caches and depots for the aid of stranded mariners in the Arctic, and for recovering a large number of documents left in cairns by early explorers, doubtless saving many of them from the effects of weather or the incursions of souvenir hunters.

One of Bernier's beacons at Winter Harbour, built in 1908 to help guide ships into the anchorage. Parks Canada/ Caroline Phillips

The trader Christian Klengenberg and his family.
Canadian Museum of Civilization/36912

While the Canadian government was busy staking its claim to the Arctic, a few hardy individuals were making their way north to settle and trade with the Inuit. Christian Klengenberg, a Danish seaman, sailed to Victoria Island in 1905 on the schooner *Olga*, laden with trade goods. He established contact with the local Inuit, who had not seen strangers since McClure and Collinson had visited more than fifty years before. In 1919 he established a permanent trading post at Rymer Point on Victoria Island, and his descendants live in the region to this day.

Others—the Hudson's Bay Company, the Canalaska Trading Company and individual traders, including a number of Inuit—built more than fifty trading posts along the shores of the western and central Arctic. Along with the traders came missionaries from the Anglican and Roman Catholic Churches, and the Mounted Police. Settlements began to spring up, with a church, a trading post, a Mounted Police detachment and the residences of the Inuit, who began to abandon their nomadic existence. In this fashion, the modern Arctic settlements of Coppermine, Holman, Cambridge Bay, Gjoa Haven and other towns were born. The waters of the Northwest Passage, once the domain of the kayak and umiak, and occasional host to the wooden ships of explorers, were now regularly plied by schooners and motor vessels operated by traders and churches. Only the Mounted Police, now renamed the Royal Canadian Mounted Police (RCMP) did not have a

The isolated Royal Canadian Mounted Police detachment at Tree River in the Arctic, 1930s. Glenbow Archives, Calgary/NA-2130-18

**The Royal Canadian Mounted
Police schooner *St. Roch*,
housed over and wintering in
at Tree River, 1930.** Vancouver
Maritime Museum/Foster Collec-
tion/HSFR-30-03a

boat. When they needed water transport, the Mounties chartered a boat or travelled as passengers, often on the HBC steamer *Nascopie*. Her captain, Robert Smellie, complained because the spurs on the Mounties' boots scuffed the decks and tore the carpets in the staterooms.

In 1927, at the instigation of Assistant Commissioner Stuart Wood of the RCMP, the force decided to build its own Arctic vessel to supply its four detachments on the 1,200-mile Arctic coast. The ship would also serve as an efficient and effective demonstration of sovereignty, as well as an extension of federal power in the north. In the winter, frozen into the ice, it would serve as the base for long patrols in the classic tradition of the force.

The Mounties' Arctic schooner was designed by Vancouver naval architect Tom Halliday. While guided by specifications from Charles Druguid, the naval constructor of the Department of the Marine in Ottawa, Halliday's primary inspiration was Roald Amundsen's Arctic schooner *Maud*. Built in 1917 for Amundsen's failed North Pole expedition, *Maud* had survived several Arctic winters locked in the ice. Sold off to satisfy Amundsen's creditors when the expedition's last try ended in 1926, *Maud* had been purchased by the Hudson's Bay Company to supply its Arctic posts. Refitted and repaired in Vancouver under Halliday's supervision, the now renamed *Baymaud*'s hearty form and layout were liberally borrowed by him when the job of designing the Mounties' schooner landed on his desk.

The Mounties' schooner was laid down at North Vancouver's Burrard Dry Dock in November 1927 and was launched in May 1928. Christened *St. Roch* for the eastern Quebec parish of St. Roch, the riding of federal Minister of Justice Ernest LaPointe, the schooner was quickly readied for her first trip north. Among the crew was newly recruited RCMP Constable Henry Asbjørn Larsen, a fourteen-year veteran of the sea, including two years as mate of Klengenberg's Arctic trading schooner *Maid of Orleans*.

St. Roch

A small, sturdy ship, *St. Roch* is just 97 feet, 6 inches long at the waterline, with a 24-foot, 9-inch beam, drawing 12 to 13 feet of water when fully loaded. The almost completely round hull, shaped like an egg, was one of the keys to the ship's success in the north.

Designed by Vancouver naval architect Tom Halliday, the hull was inspired by his examination of Roald Amundsen's "polarskib" *Maud*. The ice slipped around the thick rounded hull when *St. Roch* was squeezed; one time the ship just popped out of the water and rocked on an ice floe. But safety in the ice made for a poor sailer. One seasick Mountie complained that in heavy seas *St. Roch* behaved like a bucking bronco and "stood on her head and stood on her tail and rolled with rails under all in one motion."

St. Roch's solid construction was another boon. The hull, built of native Douglas fir, was nearly 2 feet thick, and the ship also had 13-by-7-inch floors, 3½-inch-thick ceiling planks inside the hull, 2¾-inch outer hull planks, and 1½ inch-thick ironbark (Australian gumwood) ice sheathing. The keel was an 11½-by-14-inch timber, and massive 11½-inch-thick horizontal ice beams braced the inside of the hull. Huge wrought-iron knees and braces also supported the hull, giving it added strength, while the natural flexibility of the wood provided just enough "give" for *St. Roch* to slip out of the ice. A steel "shoe" was added to the bow in 1939 to help push through ice.

Built as an auxiliary schooner, *St. Roch* had two masts when launched in 1928, but the sails were rarely used. Instead, a 150-horsepower Union diesel drove the single propeller. In 1944, just before the second trip through the Northwest Passage, a new 300-horsepower Union diesel was installed, the masts were shifted, a new ketch rig was added and a deckhouse with a large, enclosed wheelhouse atop it was built.

Although retired in 1948, *St. Roch* was sent to Halifax by way of the Panama Canal in 1950 for possible work in the eastern Arctic, making her the first ship to circumnavigate North America. Plans to use *St. Roch* in the east never materialized, and by 1952 the ship's future was uncertain. The citizens of Vancouver successfully lobbied for the return of the ship to the city of her birth, and in October 1954, with Henry Larsen at the helm, *St. Roch* triumphantly entered the harbour. Hauled ashore in April 1958, *St. Roch* formed the centrepiece of the Vancouver Maritime Museum. Housed in a distinctive A-frame in 1966 and restored to her 1944 appearance inside and out by Parks Canada, the ship is now a National Historic Site hosting thousands of visitors.

A tour through *St. Roch* is like stepping back in time. The ship is crowded with provisions for an Arctic voyage—tins of biscuits, canned goods, sacks of coal, barrels of fuel oil. The spartan, cramped cabins and forecastle are decorated with family photographs, uniforms hanging from hooks, and a book or magazine left on a bunk. The calendar on the engine room bulkhead notes that the date is September 4, 1944, and the radio broadcasts news and music from a world at war.

St. Roch is special not just for her history but for the experience she offers. The ship is a unique artifact of Arctic endurance, a compelling symbol of human endeavour in a forbidding land, and a reminder of ordinary men rendered heroic by unusual and extreme circumstances at the top of the world.

TOP *St. Roch*, frozen in and wintering next to the Hudson's Bay Company trading schooner *Nigalik*, 1936. Vancouver Maritime Museum/ St. Roch National Historic Site Collection/HSFR-30-20a

BOTTOM *St. Roch* in the ice, 1928. Vancouver Maritime Museum/St. Roch National Historic Site Collection/HSUS-20-9a

The Norwegian-born Larsen, like Amundsen before him, had grown up in sight of the sea and spent his childhood reading the accounts of explorers. Fired by tales of the Arctic and encouraged by Amundsen, whom he had met in 1924, Larsen joined the RCMP to explore the frozen seas and lands of the north. He also wanted to repeat Amundsen's feat of navigating the Northwest Passage. In 1936, Larsen told his superior: "I would like one day to proceed right through the Northwest Passage with the *St. Roch*." Larsen believed the ship was built to take it and believed that she could meet the challenge.

Henry Asbjørn Larsen

Born at Frederickstad, Norway, on September 30, 1899, Henry Asbjørn Larsen grew up fired by dreams of the sea and the north. His studies of geography and history gave him a hunger for "new lands and a curiosity for the history of the past." After an apprenticeship at sea that began at age fifteen, Larsen graduated from the Norwegian State Navigation School, served a six-month stretch of duty in the Norwegian Navy, and signed on as fourth mate of the steamer *Theodore Roosevelt*.

Roosevelt connected Norway with various Pacific coast ports, and while docked in Seattle, Washington, Larsen met polar explorer Roald Amundsen and his pilot, Oscar Omdahl. His imagination stirred by Omdahl's tales of the north, Larsen left *Theodore Roosevelt* in 1923 when the ship docked in Vancouver. The following spring, his chance to go north arrived, as the mate of trader Christian Klengenberg's schooner *Maid of Orleans*.

Larsen learned much about the Arctic from

Klengenberg. He also befriended the Royal Canadian Mounted Police constables stationed on Herschel Island, and he decided to join the RCMP, particularly if he could serve in the north. One of the Mounties, Inspector T. B. Caulkin, told Larsen that one day the force would operate a small schooner of its own for Arctic service. Returning on *Maid of Orleans* to Seattle, where he was paid off, Larsen made his way to British Columbia, working at odd jobs until the opportunity to join the RCMP arrived with the news of *St. Roch*'s construction.

Initially assigned as mate, Larsen was given command of *St. Roch* in August 1928. In 1929, he was appointed a corporal in the RCMP, and following his first epic voyage through the Northwest Passage, was promoted to staff sergeant in 1942 and later to inspector. At the time of his retirement in 1961, Larsen was the officer commanding "G" Division. In addition to professional recognition and promotion in the RCMP, Henry Larsen received many honours,

including the Polar Medal, awarded to him and his crew in 1942 by George VI, and the Royal Canadian Geographic Society's first Massey Medal.

Henry Larsen married Mary Hargreaves on February 7, 1935, in Vancouver, and they had three children. After his retirement, Henry and Mary Larsen lived for a while in Lunenberg, Nova Scotia, but in September 1964 moved to Vancouver, primarily to take charge of *St. Roch* as a museum ship.

Unfortunately, Larsen died in his sixty-fifth year, on October 29, 1964. One of his last remarks, in a letter to a friend, was that he would "soon be setting out on that last, great sled patrol."

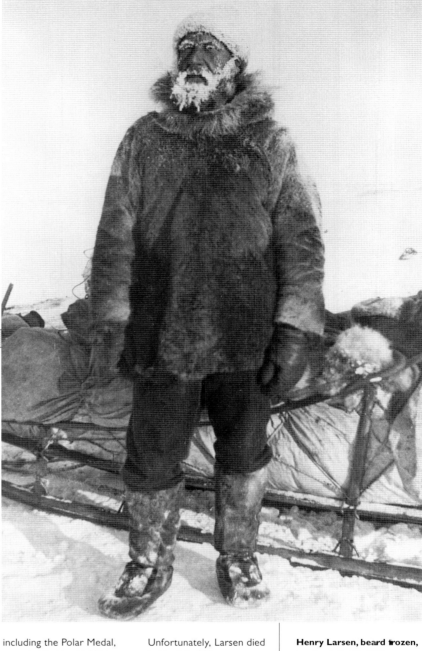

Henry Larsen, beard frozen, on dogsled patrol. Vancouver Maritime Museum/HCWO–100–13a

Baymaud (formerly *Maud*)

A forgotten wreck lies on the shores of Cambridge Bay, with the tip of the bow and a section of the starboard side rising from the water. The ice has gouged and scarred the timbers and stripped the decks of the masts, rigging and superstructure. Beneath the cold, blue-green water, the hull is intact and the interior compartments lie open to the sea. Off to one side, a mast trails down into the depths, its tip poking into the mud. A diver's hand, when it brushes against the silt and algae on the main hatch, exposes paint and the still crisp numerals denoting the ship's registration and tonnage.

This wreck is *Baymaud*, a Hudson's Bay Company supply ship and floating depot that sank here in 1930. But earlier in her career, the ship had been known as *Maud*. Built near Oslo, Norway, in 1917, *Maud* was the last sea-going command of explorer Roald Amundsen. After his conquest of the Northwest Passage in 1903–6 and his subsequent trip to the South Pole in 1911, Amundsen decided to build a ship, let it freeze into the Arctic ice, and drift to the North Pole. He made four attempts failing each time. The *Maud* expeditions bankrupted him, and after losing the ship to his creditors in 1925, Amundsen turned his attention to the opportunity to fly to the pole.

Maud was purchased by the Hudson's Bay Company and refitted as *Baymaud* under the supervision of Vancouver naval architect Tom Hall day. The ship gained a place in Arctic history when he used her lines and layout to design the Royal Canadian Mounted Police vessel *St. Roch*.

A small leak in the propeller shaft ultimately claimed *Baymaud*. Later, her half-submerged hulk was used as a mooring by *St. Roch* on more than one occasion. The wreck of *Baymaud* was surveyed in 1996 by a team from the Vancouver Maritime Museum and the Underwater Archaeological Society of British Columbia. The connection between *Baymaud* and *St. Roch* was discovered during the survey. The wreck is marked on the hamlet of Cambridge Bay's historic tour of the community, and visitors who make the trek out to the edge of the rocky shore are rewarded with a view of the weathered timbers of a ship that has a special link to the quest for the Northwest Passage, making her greatest contribution at the end of her otherwise failed career.

Roald Amundsen's former ship *Maud*, moored at Cambridge Bay as the Hudson's Bay Company depot ship *Baymaud*, sinks at her moorings in 1931. Vancouver Maritime Museum/St. Roch National Historic Site Collection/Bill White/HNOS-30-11a

The Northwest Passage Conquered 189

**Grounded ice in Dolphin and
Union Strait, as seen from
St. Roch's deck, August 1937.**
Vancouver Maritime
Museum/Frank Willan
Collection/HSVS-30-02a

The opportunity finally came in September 1939, when the RCMP authorized Larsen to make the Northwest Passage trip. *St. Roch* was to sail the passage from west to east, then travel on to Halifax. *St. Roch* would be the first ship to complete the passage since Amundsen's *Gjøa*, and "ours would be the first ship to conquer the Northwest passage in that direction." For Larsen, "Here it was. My great moment. Canada was at war and the government had realized the need to demonstrate the country's sovereignty over the Arctic islands."

St. Roch put into the Canadian naval base at Esquimalt, near Victoria, on Vancouver Island, for repairs to make her ready for the passage. Wartime exigencies meant that Larsen would not get the new, more powerful diesel engine he had asked for, but a new auxiliary was added to recharge the ship's batteries. The bow was sheathed in steel to better withstand the ice.

Larsen selected a southern route through the passage, following much of Amundsen's track. A devoted student of Arctic history, Larsen packed a number of books from his personal library to take on the voyage, among them an English first edition of Amundsen's account of *Gjøa*'s voyage. He constantly referred to it and his other books during the two-year trip.

St. Roch, the intent of her voyage a wartime secret, sailed from Vancouver in the early morning hours of June 23, 1940. On July 4, the ship cleared Unimak Pass and entered the Bering Sea, reaching Point Barrow on July 23. It was a bad year for ice. Larsen had a difficult time dodging ice floes as he pushed past Barrow and on to Herschel Island. From there, he sailed to Cambridge Bay, the ship's usual winter quarters. Larsen had hoped to reach Gjoa Haven, but, as he noted, "it was too late in the season." The thick ice, and the fear of being frozen in at a bad spot where the pack ice might push the ship ashore and crush it, sent *St. Roch* westward in retreat. Finally, the ship stopped at Walker Bay, on the western shores of Victoria Island. There,

300 feet from shore, the ship froze into winter quarters in September.

St. Roch broke out of the ice on the morning of July 31, 1941. Instead of continuing east, the ship received orders to head west to Tuktoyaktuk. Wartime shortages of transportation and the traditional duties of the RCMP called. After ferrying supplies from Tuktoyaktuk to the communities of Coppermine and Cambridge Bay, Larsen was able to turn east once more on August 19. Slowly working through the ice, he rounded the southern end of King William Island and reached Gjoa Haven on August 27.

Although the ice was moving south, Larsen decided to push north against it. He soon realized that the ship was in danger. Heading toward the Boothia Peninsula and the only safe moorage he knew from his readings, Pasley Bay, marked on an 1855 Admiralty chart, Larsen arrived on September 3 and dropped anchor. The ice closed in, trapping *St. Roch* and forcing her down the bay, the weight of the ice overpowering the engines. An opening in the ice brought temporary relief, but when Larsen anchored in the open patch of water, the wind shifted. *St. Roch* was pinned between heavy floes, helplessly drifting with the ice.

The ship hit a submerged shoal and grounded. A lighter, smaller vessel, like *Gjøa*, would have been overwhelmed and crushed. But the thick, rounded hull of *St. Roch* pivoted twice, as she was thrown to port and then to starboard. Ice pushed up over the starboard side and began to fall onto the deck. "I wondered if we had come this far to be crushed like a nut on a shoal and then buried by the ice," Larsen wrote. The ship nearly rolled onto her side, dragging her anchors, when she suddenly popped free.

Larsen managed to hook a wire rope to a rock in the bay. With this, and 1,600 pounds of steel anchors laid out all the way at the end of 90 fathoms (540 feet) of chain, the ship stopped. Nearly ashore, *St. Roch* froze in for the winter. The Mounties used the interlude to patrol the

Boothia Peninsula and King William Island. Tragedy struck when Constable Albert "Frenchy" Chartrand, an old Arctic hand and crew member, died of an apparent heart attack in February 1942. Larsen and an Inuk guide, Equalla, made a 1,140-mile dogsled journey to bring a priest back to the ship for a funeral service. Chartrand was buried on a nearby hill overlooking the bay, with a 15-foot-high stone cairn to mark the spot. It stands there still.

On August 3, 1942, fearing they would be stuck for another winter, Larsen broke out of Pasley Bay and re-entered the thick ice. Caught again by the floes, with *St. Roch*'s stern out of the water and the bow going under, Larsen blasted her free with explosives. He moved on, ramming the ice and forcing his way into narrow leads. "Thus," he reported, "little by little, the *St. Roch* made headway."

"I got the feeling that I had constantly to match wits with the moving pack ice," Larsen later recalled. "Many a time did I head for an opening in the ice only to watch it crash together just ahead of me, as if it were a living thing deliberately trying to keep me from reaching open water. On other occasions the ice would snap shut behind me, as if it held me in a trap. But it also happened that when things looked hopeless and I was almost resigned to giving up, the ice would suddenly open up . . . and . . . the leads would gradually get wider and wider and allow us to slide through the cracks for mile after mile."

On August 12, one of the engine cylinders cracked, and with partial power—at a time when the schooner needed everything she had—they crawled up the Boothia coast to reach Bellot Strait on August 29. It had taken them twenty-five days to make 60 miles. "We had almost reached the point where we were going to congratulate each other in our good fortune," wrote Larsen. Instead, as the ship entered the 18-mile-

St. Roch, **sheathed with ice blocks for insulation while wintering in.** Glenbow Archives, Calgary/NA-2821-7

long, mile-wide strait, she was almost wrecked. Ice racing up the strait had jammed up against an ice floe that was stuck on a submerged reef. Larsen ordered full speed and rammed the floe, only to stop dead in the water. The ice began to pile up behind *St. Roch*, which, wedged tight, was squeezed by incredible pressure. The timbers groaned as "huge cakes of ice spun and gyrated in large whirlpools. In some of the whirlpools we could see narwhals, lost and bewildered, with their long spiralled horns waving in the air as they stood almost upright in the water."

For nearly an hour the ship remained stuck in the ice. Then, suddenly, the floe, pack ice and schooner broke free and drifted out of the strait. A relieved Larsen anchored *St. Roch* at the Hudson Bay Company's trading post of Fort Ross, at the eastern end of the strait. From there, to leave the Arctic Ocean, they headed up Prince Regent Inlet to Barrow Strait and the settlement of Pond Inlet, where the dogs and much of the ship's gear were landed. Larsen and his crew now prepared for the final leg south to Halifax, where they arrived at 3:30 in the afternoon of October 11, 1942.

"It had not been an easy trip," Larsen reported in his typically understated fashion. The three seasons he had just spent on the passage were the worst years he had seen in the Arctic, and "without hesitation I would say that most ships encountering the conditions we faced would have failed." After a respite that included the installation of a new, larger engine and a new pilothouse on deck, Larsen and *St. Roch* were ready for a return trip through the passage to Vancouver. This time, Larsen decided to take "the more northerly route, through Lancaster Sound and west to Melville Island and then across McClure Strait to Prince of Wales Strait. This was the real Northwest Passage, I felt, and it had never before been navigated." Only Sir Edward Parry had come close, in 1819.

After two false starts, Larsen left late in the season on July 26, 1944. Arriving at Pond Inlet

Blasting the Ice

Occasionally, ships trapped in the Arctic ice used explosives to blast their way out. The Royal Navy expeditions used black powder charges, as did the Royal Canadian Mounted Police. Henry Larsen, writing in his autobiography, *The Big Ship*, explained how the explosives were used:

> The charges were made up of about five pounds of black powder in a bottle, made watertight with Sunlight soap. We then inserted a fuse in the top and tied the bottle to a long pole. At the Naval Dockyards I had obtained a dozen or so long rods used for cleaning the large naval guns, and being fifteen to twenty feet long, they were ideal for our purpose. Before we lit the fuse, we had to find a suitable opening between the ice-floes so that the charge could be shoved down . . . [and] explode a few feet below the ice.

> It was dangerous work. Once, a pole slid back up out of the ice, and Larsen realized the charge was about to explode next to where he was standing:

> There was nothing else for me to do but grab the pole and push it back down as far as I could and keep it down until it exploded. I was showered with water and small chunks of ice and it gave me an uncomfortable feeling to see the red flame through the ice under me.

Portrait of Henry Larsen aboard *St. Roch*, 1944.
Vancouver Maritime Museum/Michael Paris

Sounding with the lead line from *St. Roch*. Vancouver Maritime Museum/St. Roch National Historic Site Collection/HCSW-100-a

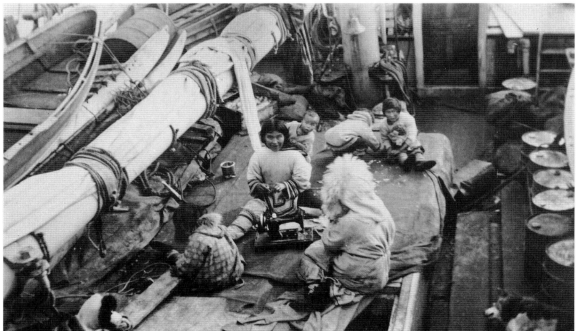

The Panippakussuk (Panipi-takochoo) family living on *St. Roch*'s main hatch cover, 1944. Vancouver Maritime Museum/St. Roch National Historic Site Collection/HISG-40-0a

on August 13, Larsen hired Inuk guide and hunter Joe Panippakussuk, who came aboard with his six-member family and seventeen dogs.

Sailing from Pond Inlet on August 17, St. Roch anchored off Beechey Island three days later. Always the Arctic scholar, Larsen went ashore to visit the site of Franklin's winter quarters. Like Amundsen before him, Larsen felt that he was on hallowed ground. Throughout his Arctic career, Larsen stopped to visit the sites of the earlier explorers and to collect relics. "Tribute is . . . due to those early explorers," he explained, because "their sacrifices and exploits blazed most of the trail we took." By the end of August, *St. Roch* stood off the entrance to McClure Strait: "We were now in waters never before sailed by any vessel." Carefully weaving through the ice, down into Prince of Wales Strait, within a few days *St. Roch* reached Walker Bay, the site of the ship's winter quarters in 1940–41.

They had essentially conquered the passage, but, mindful of the ice, Larsen pushed on. The ship rode out a savage winter storm at Tuktoyaktuk, then carried on to Herschel Island, where the Panippakussuk family was landed. Now came the final race with the ice to reach Point Barrow.

St. Roch won the race and on September 27 passed through the Bering Strait. On October 16, 1944, *St. Roch* arrived in Vancouver harbour after an absence of four years. Larsen, the first man to traverse the Northwest Passage in both directions, had also made the northern run in an amazing eighty-six days. He, his crew and the dauntless little Mountie schooner were feted in the press and awarded numerous honours and medals. Larsen quietly accepted these accolades while readying his ship for a return to the Arctic and to regular duties as a police boat. Larsen and *St. Roch*'s incredible feat would never be forgotten by the Canadian people. They had conquered the fabled Northwest Passage twice, and, in doing so, had ensured recognition of Canadian sovereignty in the north.

The Passage After 1945

If our naval frontiers are to be the enemies' coast line and if we are to maintain control of the seas, then we are obliged to extend our present capability to include the Arctic. —COMMODORE O. C. S. ROBERTSON, ROYAL CANADIAN NAVY, 1960

EVEN AS *St. Roch* made her two transits through the Northwest Passage, the Arctic was changing. It was, like the rest of the world, being drawn into war. German weather stations in the Arctic, between East Greenland and Norway, were broadcasting reports to the Luftwaffe and Kriegsmarine. German U-boats were pushing at the edge of the ice as they lay in wait for merchant convoys on the northern runs.

By the end of the war, when *St. Roch* returned to police duties in the Arctic in 1945–46, the modern age had arrived. In the winter, the

majority of the ship's crew were flown out of the Arctic. As well, *St. Roch* was visited by troops participating in Operation Muskox, a combined Canadian-American operation to test military equipment in Arctic conditions. The Cold War had also begun, bringing substantial change to the north. Starting in the late 1940s, the Arctic skies filled with the contrails of long-range bombers, and later, the tracks of Intercontinental Ballistic Missiles (ICBMS), making the far north the strategic frontier of the Cold War. In 1955, the construction of a series of radar stations— the Distant Early Warning system, or the DEW line, began. The arrival of the military brought even more changes as bases were built and personnel settled in.

The next ship to sail through the Northwest Passage was a Royal Canadian Navy vessel, HMCS *Labrador*, under the command of C. C. S.

FACING PAGE Iceberg and surf, Devon Island. Corel

BELOW *St. Roch* tied up next to the larger HMCS *Labrador*, which also sailed the Northwest passage, at Esquimalt, British Columbia, 1955. Vancouver Maritime Museum/no number

HMCS *Labrador* **in the
Northwest Passage, 1954.**
Maritime Museum of British
Columbia

Robertson. She made the trip in 1954, pushing west through Lancaster Sound, Barrow Strait, Viscount Melville Sound and then, following Larsen's track of 1944, through Prince of Wales Strait, then west from Amundsen Gulf and out through Bering Strait. The first naval ship to navigate the passage, *Labrador* was a harbinger of things to come. As Commodore Robertson noted: "It is our misfortune that we must now look to the Arctic, not just as a source of future resources, but as an immediate defence against possible aggression. We must define the place that the Arctic could, or might have to play in the defence of the North American Continent."

The next strategic step was the introduction of the submarine. The idea of submarines penetrating the ice cap and navigating in the north dated back to the nineteenth century, when Jules Verne's Captain Nemo and his *Nautilus* did so in *20,000 Leagues Beneath the Sea*. Early efforts to navigate under the ice included Sir Hubert Wilkins's 1931 attempt in the former United States submarine *O-12*, renamed *Nautilus*, postwar United States Navy experiments in 1946 as part of Operation Nanook, and a 1952 cruise by USS *Redfish* to McClure Strait. The keys to success were the development of the nuclear-powered submarine in the 1950s, forward- and upward-ranging sonar, and a fair measure of good old-fashioned bold endeavour and luck. The USS *Nautilus*, the first nuclear submarine, reached 90° north on August 5, 1958. The nuclear submarine USS *Skate* was the next north, followed by USS *Sargo*. Then, in 1960, USS *Seadragon*, with George P. Steele in

Crew members from USS *Seadragon* gather on the ice, as viewed through the submarine's periscope. Naval Historical Center, Washington, D.C./USN-1050048

command, made the first submerged transit of the Northwest Passage. Steele, much like his predecessors, had to feel his way through in spots. After reaching the Beaufort Sea on August 21, 1960, *Seadragon* headed up to the North Pole before leaving the Arctic.

Commodore O. C. S. Robertson of the Royal Canadian Navy sailed aboard *Seadragon* on this historic voyage. In a confidential report, he noted: "The nuclear submarine has demonstrated its ability to traverse the Arctic Ocean at will. . . . It has also demonstrated its ability to transit narrow and shallow channels submerged under the seas' ice cover. . . . The borders for which

nature had previously provided a sure defense are no longer protected. The Arctic is a highway if we will but have the wit to use it." Military and naval planners agreed; to this day, the Arctic is regularly patrolled by the nuclear submarines of the United States and Russia—and perhaps other nations. American, Canadian and Russian ice-breakers also work the same waters, though in the post-Cold War period, the Russian icebreak-ers carry tourists, not commissars and naval personnel.

The current use of the Arctic is not strategic but commercial. The discovery of rich natural resources in the north has spurred development,

Commander George P. Steele of USS *Seadragon* celebrates the first submerged transit of the Northwest Passage at a press conference. Naval Historical Center, Washington, D.C./no number

new settlements and more regular use of the waters of the Northwest Passage. A rich oil discovery in 1968 at Prudhoe Bay, on Alaska's North Slope, inspired the Humble Oil & Refining Company—the domestic subsidiary of Standard Oil—to attempt the first commercial voyage through the Northwest Passage, hoping to find a relatively short, fast route from the oil fields to refineries in the eastern United States. The 155,000-ton tanker ss *Manhattan* was refitted as an icebreaker and sent through the passage in 1969. Escorted by the Canadian icebreaker *John A. Macdonald*, *Manhattan* made it to Melville Island. The ice of McClure Strait thwarted the huge ship, however, and *Manhattan* ended up following Larsen and Robertson's track through Prince of Wales Strait, reaching open water on September 14, 1969. The achievement was heralded as a "forerunner of a fleet of icebreaker-tankers that might make use of Arctic waters a commonplace within less than a decade."

The icebreaker-tankers did not follow. But since then, dozens of other ships have made the passage, some following the coast in the wake of Amundsen, others in the deep-water straits. They have included steel yachts, modern kayaks, Canadian Coast Guard icebreakers, cruise ships and a motor-powered traditional skin umiak.

The tanker *Manhattan* breaks ice on the first commercial transit of the Northwest Passage, 1969.
Vancouver Maritime Museum/7084

Tourists at the edge of the ice, 1990s. Nunavut Tourism

The fabled Northwest Passage, so many centuries in the finding, in the end proved neither a fast road to the riches of the Orient, nor an easy route for the explorer seeking fame. It traverses a difficult land, a land that is experiencing, at the dawn of the twenty-first century, great change. The natural resources of the Arctic are spurring new development, even as the Cold War has ended and the military withdraws and the DEW line stations are dismantled. The Inuit, who have lived here longer than anyone, have been seriously affected. The forced relocation of people to establish Canadian claims to isolated regions, as well as the cultural changes wrought by a consumer-based society imposed on the North, have brought damage to the Inuit. Yet they survive, and in 1999 gained back a measure of self-government and a reassertion that these are their lands with the Canadian government's decision to create the semi-autonomous region of Nunavut.

For all the triumph and tragedy that have transpired, the the Northwest Passage through the Arctic will be remembered as one of the great landmarks of the human heart. And, in those isolated places, the wind still howls, the ice shifts, and the tendrils of snow drift around bleached bones and rusted tins.

List of Maps